TARGET FOR TONIGHT

TARGET FOR TONIGHT

Flying Long-range Reconnaissance
and
Pathfinder Missions in World War II

The Memoirs of
Squadron Leader Denys A. Braithwaite, DFC*

Pen & Sword
AVIATION

First published in Great Britain in 2005 by
Pen & Sword Aviation
an imprint of
Pen & Sword Books Ltd

ISBN 1 84415 159 X

A CIP catalogue record for this book is
available from the British Library

Typeset in Palatino by
Phoenix Typesetting, Auldgirth, Dumfriesshire

Printed and bound in England by
CPI UK

Pen & Sword Books Ltd incorporates the Imprints of Pen & Sword Aviation,
Pen & Sword Maritime, Pen & Sword Military, Wharncliffe Local History,
Pen & Sword Select, Pen & Sword Military Classics and Leo Cooper.

For a complete list of Pen & Sword titles please contact
PEN & SWORD BOOKS LIMITED
47 Church Street, Barnsley, South Yorkshire, S70 2AS, England
E-mail: enquiries@pen-and-sword.co.uk
Website: www.pen-and-sword.co.uk

Contents

CHAPTER ONE

608 Squadron

The war is long over, it is a fine sunny day in the early seventies. I was looking out of the windows of my house at the end of a pleasant, tree-lined road in Kensington. An old air force friend, one of the few remaining, telephoned last night after what transpired to be sixteen years, and he is coming to spend the day with me. He is now a Jesuit priest, so I was watching for a figure in a brown habit with a long cord dangling to the ground from his waist, walking up the pavement. I wonder after all this time whether he would be striding out or shuffling along. I think monks do either. He used to look like Just Jake, from one of the national Newspapers comic strips, who was the racecourse con-man, always with a bent cigarette dangling out of his mouth, only Jerker never smoked that I can remember. Of course, he might be thin on top now or have a bald pate instead of the rakish, slightly untidy straight black hair that used to go back across his head.

Whilst awaiting his arrival I might as well relate back to yesterday evening. The telephone rang at 6 p.m. and my wife answered. 'Can I speak to Denys, please? I have the right number, I hope,' said the voice.

'Who are you?' my wife naturally asked.

'It's Jerker here. You're not his wife are you? I remember her but you have a different voice.'

'Jerker,' repeated my wife. 'Yes I've heard him talk about you, but he thinks you are probably dead. I'll go and get him. He'll be very pleased to hear from you. You are right, I'm not the same wife you remember. Just a moment.'

With that, my wife came out into the garden. 'Don't get a shock, but one of your old colleagues seems to have just returned from outer space. Jerker is on the phone for you.'

I picked up the phone. 'Jerker,' I said, 'where on earth have you come from? A quick calculation tells me it's the better part of twenty years since you disappeared without trace.'

'Sixteen, to be precise, old lad.' He went on, 'Do you remember I was working for Shell Oil up in Cheshire amongst the bosoms of my elderly female relatives when I last came to see you? That was the weekend we were working out the specifications for the bride you thought I ought to acquire, good RC, a bit of money, not too much, good looks, not too many, and limitless tolerance.' I remembered, it suddenly seemed like yesterday. My earlier second wife had argued that the good RC restricted the field by at least 50 per cent, but Jerker had been most adamant. 'Well,' he went on,' you see, I hadn't been back many days when I made one of those unfortunate slip-ups that affect your life. A garage wanted some more petrol and inadvertently I sent a tanker of diesel. Shell were not very understanding about it. I chucked it in and the same day presented myself before their local holinesses, gave them my collection of antique-pub title deeds, which were really quite valuable, and they have been looking after me ever since. Unfortunately, you may think the Jesuit order that I have joined requires pretty severe initiation, including sixteen years of total silence. That has now come to an end.'

'My God, Jerker, then where are you now and can you come to see us?'

'Oh, yes, that's what I'm ringing up about, I'm now the bursar at a teaching college in north London. You see, I'm not a fully qualified Jesuit, never will be, but this bursar's job and such like are reserved for people like me, and of course, very important, all the twenty odd teachers I have here are all ex-operational types, air force, army, submariners, you name it, we've got them. A terrific bunch of people. Oh, and by the way, I am now called Brother Norman.'

'That's fine, Jerker, but you haven't answered, when can you come to see us?'

'Is there any chance I could come tomorrow?'

And, so it was, that I was waiting by the window for Wing Commander Norman Jackson-Smith, DFC, otherwise known as Jerker, now Brother Norman.

An immaculate white Ford saloon came up the street, hesitated and then pulled into the parking space between the front of my house and the road. Out stepped a most immaculate Jerker, in grey Savile Row suit, smart shirt, tie and impeccable black shoes.

Formalities over and drinks in hand, I started to enquire about all this. 'Oh, it's simple,' says Jerker. 'I tell them I'm going out and I get issued with a car, all spotlessly clean, too. I have to elect whether it's an expensive outing I'm going on or not so much. There are three categories, twenty pounds, ten pounds and five pounds. I told them', and my wife interrupted as he repeated 'them' again, 'who is them?', and in any event 'them' didn't want any of the twenty pounds back. As for the suit, they sent me to Savile Row for this, and if and when it gets worn out, they will send me for another.'

We sat there enraptured, absorbing all this.Then, Jerker asked what we had in mind for the afternoon. My wife suggested that often on a Saturday afternoon we watched the television racing. 'Oh, yes please,' said Jerker, 'just what I hoped you might say.'

We had lunch and in due course it came time to get the newspapers out to decide what horses to put our modest bets on with the well-known bookmaker who was glad to give me the facility of an account because, as is the nature of things, we almost always lost.

'I'm going to have a pound on Welsh Fool in the first,' said my wife. 'What do you want, Jerker?'

'Oh, I don't bet, I'm not allowed to, actually,' replied Jerker, 'but if you don't mind me saying so, I know you've chosen a short-priced horse with a good jockey, but I think Crocodile Heaven will win this race.'

'But, Jerker, that's quoted here at twenty to one,' said my wife. She rang the bookie and put her pound on Welsh Fool.

The race began and Crocodile Heaven won easily, by at least two lengths and Jerker felt quite excited and pleased with himself. 'Well, Jerker, what do you think about the next race?' we asked.

'Oh, I'm not absolutely certain, but I think Catamaran has a very good chance, and he's not carrying any weight to speak of.'

'But, Jerker, that's even worse, it's twenty-five to one,' said my wife. 'Surely Brown Bit must be a better bet.' The household money went on Brown Bit, and again we settled down to watch the race. Catamaran led into the straight and at the two furlong marker had demolished all the opposition.

'Look here, Jerker,' I said, 'this is just not possible. One is astonishing enough, but two in a row, amazing!'

'Look,' said Jerker, suddenly beginning to sound apologetic I've told you all about this silence business. Part of it is several hours a day kneeling down and praying. I'm just not very good at praying, so I keep myself occupied, I've been studying *Time Form* for the last sixteen years!'

That meant that it was about twenty years since I had written to Jerker from my hospital in India to ask him if he would like me to nominate him to take over the Mosquito force I had been going to lead in the forthcoming attack on Penang and Singapore. He had written back to me to explain that he was now commanding one of Max Aitkin's Wing of Mosquito Squadrons at Banff. He had gone on to describe his last operation in the European war. The Wing had taken off for the Norwegian coast where it had been met by a large force of JU 88s. At this time they were radioed from base to return home as the war had officially ended at 11am. So, they knew it, but it was pretty obvious that the Germans didn't, and a great dog fight ensued, more frightening to Jerker than almost any other as the last thing he wanted was to be shot down when the war was over.

The two of us went on reminiscing till hours after Jerker should have left, but it was then that it occurred to me that the history of ones own part of the war ought to be recorded, and then and there I started to write my story, starting from the very beginning.

I think it is time that I explained how I became involved in the Royal Air force. We were a Yorkshire family and my father, who had fought gallantly in the trenches in the First World War, had become MP for an east Yorkshire constituency in 1927. My mother, who was American, was never at ease in England and spent much time in the USA. In 1938, I was trying very hard to secure my position as hooker in our school rugby team. In the trial for the great match of the season I charged down the opposing full back and badly damaged my leg, laying me off both the rugger and the following term's field sports completely. I had already passed matriculation and at the end of term had gone up to Trinity College Cambridge to sit the Littlego examination, entitling me to go up to Cambridge the following October. Not being academically inclined, however, I did not want to spend the intervening two terms at school, and got my parents' consent to leave.

Father persuaded me to go to work in his very grotty coal mine at Huddersfield, and I must say at a salary that even the office petty cash would not have noticed. I lodged with the mine manager and his family, and at the weekend, used to drive a five pound purchase 1929 Riley Nine to my grandparents' home between Leeds and Wetherby.

Grandfather's home was a splendid establishment. Although he never said so, he clearly did not think the Riley Nine mingled too well with his other higher-class cars. Also, he was not over enthused when I frequently rang for Buckborough, his chauffeur, to come and get me going again when I sat stranded on the road between Huddersfield and Wetherby. He diplomatically suggested that if it was agreeable he would buy me a more reliable car. I had seen a magnificent second-hand SS Jaguar in a car showroom in Leeds. They wanted £150 for it, so Grandfather drove down to see it with me. The salesman was told to start it up, but he could not get the engine started. Grandfather put his large Yorkshire foot down: 'we're not wasting time around here, lad.' With that he took me up the road to Appleyards in the Headrow and paid £155 for a new bright-red open Ford Prefect, not quite an SS Jaguar, but it was a flashy colour and could reasonably be guaranteed to start.

I had cousins, God bless them, who did not think Father had done too well for me in the coal mine, and who felt that they could offer a better solution for me at the weekends than staying with my elderly grandparents. They introduced me to the Auxiliary Air Force.

My mother was in the USA when I asked Father to sign the papers allowing me to join on my eighteenth birthday. He signed with alacrity but said, 'don't tell your mother I did this for you!'

From then on life became much better. I was paid about 7s 6d (37½p) a day for Saturdays and Sundays and had a mileage allowance of 6d (2½p) a mile from Thornaby aerodrome to my grandparents' home, maximum allowable fifty miles each way, actual forty-nine miles. I was also allowed to fill up at Grandfather's garage pump in the yard, so I had suddenly become moderately rich! My income had actually quadrupled.

We were an intake of five new pilots that summer. Philip Cunliffe-Lister, whose father was the squadron's honorary Air Commodore, and who had already amassed quite a few hours in his university air squadron, me and three others.

The fact that the object of the squadron was to fly aeroplanes was somewhat secondary to me and I soon realised that I was considerably dismayed at the idea of flying, so much so that after more than twelve hours of dual instruction, divided amongst most of the competent pilots in the squadron, everybody became a bit bored. One evening, standing on the tarmac, I asked Flight Lieutenant Harold Allsopp, our Senior Instructor and Squadron Adjutant, 'What percentage of fatalities occur on first solos?' Harold replied, 'Not many.' That was not the answer I was hoping for, and I did not go solo that weekend either.

Eventually the dreaded day caught up with me. I had to go, and it was an event that a good many of the squadron turned out to watch. It was a gorgeous midsummer afternoon, with a slight breeze from the west rippling through the top of the long grass. I was desperately sorry that I was not going to be able to enjoy it very much longer. At the maximum, until the fuel ran out, I reckoned I had an hour and a half. The aircraft was an Avro Tutor, a very gentlemanly plane on which I had been training. I had a lot of confidence in it, but absolutely none in myself. I strapped in, started up, and taxied out across the grass. On and on across the field I went, way down to the far corner, turned into the wind, took a last look around, opened the throttle – and that was it. The wheels came off the ground and I was in the air. I realised I was perfectly all right, and I was pleased as punch about the whole thing.

I circuited out away from the bottom end of the field, and, as I came around, I looked across at all the chaps standing watching on the tarmac. I knew what they were waiting for – a good bounce when I came down. There was a dip right over on the far side away from them where I could touch down out of sight, and down I came into it. Throttle back, stick back, it was a perfect landing. I was quite upset that they would never know that I had made a three-pointer first time. However, in all fairness, I should have done after thirteen and a half hours dual! I taxied in pretty pleased with myself all the same.

After this sword of Damocles had been lifted from my head, those wonderful days of summer 1939 passed quite blissfully. Everybody put in the most flying hours they could in preparation for the summer camp in the last two weeks of August. Then I would be able to say goodbye to the dreadful old coal mine, the clogs, the acetylene lamps, the grime and the mud, and go off to camp at Warmwell in Dorset.

Warmwell was between Weymouth and Bournemouth. Weymouth was an important naval base with a large flotilla of submarines. The squadron had been converted from a fighter squadron on Hawker Demons to a Coastal Command squadron on Ansons. Most of the senior squadron pilots had never flown twin-engined aircraft before, so their time was divided between putting in flying hours on Ansons and going to Weymouth to spend the day in submarines, as air defence against submarines in particular was now to be the squadron's role. For us newcomers, it involved just putting in hours on our training aircraft. Every time it was my turn, I would set off to find the old man of Cerne Abbas, a chalk effigy amongst the hillsides not far away. But, I knew virtually nothing about navigation. I never did find it, but what was worse, I had the utmost difficulty in finding my aerodrome again afterwards, which would put me late back on the ground, much to the fury of whoever else was next to go out.

In the evenings, we would drive into Bournemouth, behaving quite scandalously. We would drive along the front, trailing blown up condoms, and one night one of our number went straight through a glass showcase in the Branksome Towers, from which we were thereafter expelled.

The atmosphere was changing, however. Suddenly, the destroyers in the harbour were taking the smart brass caps off their big guns. Our people would go down to the harbour for the day's sailing with the submarines, only to find that they had vanished overnight. Hitler invaded Poland and on 23 August the signal came through: 'All units return immediately to war stations.' It turned out that our war station was where we had come from: Thornaby-on-Tees.

As we were under canvas, all the tents had to come down, to be stowed away along with the rest of our gear into the Ansons, and then, in the afternoon, one after another, the aircraft took off. As each Anson accelerated down the grass runway parallel to the main road, the crowds who had gathered along the aerodrome fence cheered and threw their hats in the air. It generated a great feeling of nostalgia.

The Assistant Adjutant, Pilot Officer Morris, who was also our junior flying instructor, had been designated, with me, to remain behind with two Tutors to collect anything that remained and return to Thornaby-on-Tees the following day. As it turned out, the weather became very poor and we struggled to make Upavon, the RAF Central Flying School, that night. The following morning the weather had further worsened. I knew nothing about navigation or map-reading; indeed, I had no maps, so Morris told me to stay tight close to him. We proceeded northwards. After twenty minutes or so, much to my relief, Morris turned back and we landed again at Upavon.

The next day, with the weather even worse, we tried again. In the Midlands I suddenly lost Morris and panic gripped me. With only sixty hours' flying experience, at 200 feet in near fog conditions and no earthly idea where I was, I was scared. Risking a collision, as he had only been 50 feet away off my right wing, I turned quite a bit in towards him and, after agonizing seconds, he suddenly appeared again out of the murk. By Nottingham, he had had enough and we landed after an hour and a half flying at Hucknall. Later the same day we tried again for Thornaby but were back on the ground again at Hucknall in fifteen minutes. Then, to my relief, Morris gave up and we ingloriously caught a train.

On the morning of 3 September, Neville Chamberlain made his announcement that a state of war would exist between Britain and Germany at 11.00 unless Hitler agreed to withdraw from Poland – which we all knew would not happen. Geoffrey Shaw, our Squadron Commander, had ordered all officers into our mess to hear Chamberlain, and suddenly we all realised we were actually at war. The joke in the squadron had been: 'If

we thought there was going to be a war, we wouldn't be here.'
As auxiliaries, it had been a super weekend club. Now, at 11.05
it was all different. And I suppose we were all proud, albeit very
apprehensive, to be there.

'Everybody on twenty-four-hour leave this minute,' said
Geoffrey Shaw. 'Get the hell out of here before the Station
Commander orders the camp gates closed. Pick up all the things
you need for a permanent stay here and be back by lunch-time
tomorrow.' There was a hectic exodus and in minutes we were
all on our way to our respective homes.

My open Ford Prefect could manage 75mph and I had
covered the 50 miles to my grandfather's home, by lunch. When
I arrived, in uniform, I was astonished to see my father there,
dressed in an exceedingly tight army uniform, with his First
World War DSO, MC, Great War campaign medals and
American Silver Star decorating it. As a territorial major he had
passed out second in Staff College in 1927, and he told us he was
going to be gazetted a major-general and would be going to the
war too. My grandparents were inordinately proud of both of us
and we all passed a most memorable and moving day together.
I returned to Thornaby the following morning with everything I
could possibly want and more, including even my father's First
World War Colt 45 with his name engraved on it.

The next morning I was awake very early and whilst it was
still dark, I drove out past Saltburn on to the cliffs above Redcar.
I got out of the car and walked to the edge of the 200 feet cliffs
to watch the sun slowly emerge above the horizon and eventually unveil an endless pool of lazily swelling grey-blue sea. Even
gulls took their time to begin their day's cliff flying and there
was nothing but stillness and a depth of tranquillity. This
was my equivalent of going before an altar to pray for the
future, only different. I was not praying to God for help, but
the sensation of solitude and contemplation was a sort of
communion for me.

Whether we won or lost was not the point. We were British.
We were honour bound through heritage to lend support to a
neighbour who was being savagely attacked and plundered by
the descendant of Attila the Hun.

I wondered about my father, thinking what a great general he
would make, about my grandparents who had already gone

through all the apprehension of their son at the front through the First World War. I wondered if my brother, who now lived in America, and all my cousins over there would come to help us, as they had in that earlier war. I wondered if our planes would be a match for the hordes of German aeroplanes, dive-bombing Stukas and the rest, that were already laying carnage all about them in Poland. And I wondered finally, just how long this incredible tranquillity and the beauty of that September morning would remain so superbly encompassing everything at that moment.

The sun was well up, its extra warmth striking into the body. The gulls were swooping and diving and uttering their cries as always, reminding me that they knew nothing of all this – this would not affect their world. I was standing where there was no war and it was time to get back to where I belonged, and where there was one.

The days of Tutor flying were over. The squadron was assigned coastal patrol duties and I was put on concentrated dual flying and low-level bombing practice. I soloed on the Anson by 12 September. Every second or third day I was made station Orderly Officer, which meant that I wore a red OO band on my left arm and roved around the camp, visiting prisoners, visiting other ranks' mess halls to ask if there were any complaints about the food and, at night in particular, touring the sentry posts. The aerodrome guard consisted of a hastily recruited batch of Old Contemptibles who all lived in the vicinity. Their contract was for two hours on, two hours off. At certain times this made life quite hazardous. As soon as they went off duty, they walked straight over the road to the local and stayed there drinking till it was their turn again. The more they drank, the more determined they were that they would defend the aerodrome against all-comers. An old drunk farm labourer with a loaded rifle and a bayonet on the end of it, prob-ably slightly deaf, can be quite a menace in the dark, particularly if he gets to thinking that you might be the enemy. At 'Alt, Oo goes there?' it was as well to do just what you were told, and quickly. Even that sometimes was not enough. One evening, one member of our squadron drove up to the main camp gate in his car, and stopped on receiving the customary challenge. The guard then proceeded without further ado to make a ferocious bayonet charge on the poor car. His aim was good and he stuck the bayonet right through one of the front tyres.

Luckily, the Station Commander would not allow the old boys on aeroplane guard around the dispersal points at night. Otherwise the Orderly Officer's job would have been more dangerous than any operational flying. As it was, the dispersal guards were drawn from the squadron NCO flying crew. One night, at about 03.00, I was on my rounds down at a remote point on the far side of the airfield, when there was a gruff 'Is that you, Orderly Officer?' I recognised the Station Commander's voice. I went through the formality of challenging him, as I knew from past experience that, if I did not I would get an almighty strip torn off. 'I'll come around with you the rest of the way,' he said. We approached the next picket. There was no challenge. The Group Captain walked right on and into the tent. There was Warrant Officer Ison, a gunner from 'A' Flight, fast asleep. 'Put this man under close arrest for sleeping on guard duty on active service,' ordered the Group Captain.

Poor Ison! When I brought him out of his cell the next morning and escorted him to the Station Commander's office, he was panic stricken. I reassured him. 'The Groupie will probably give you a damn good ticking off and confine you to camp for a week,' I said. How wrong I was. 'The sentence for what you have done is death,' said the Group Captain. 'We are at war now and I propose that everybody shall realise that. Take him back to his cell.' I was shaken to the core, but that was nothing compared with the effect it had on Ison. The war had scarcely been going three weeks and nobody had seen a thing so far, except the Old Contemptibles. How could this happen to him, a married man with three children? The station prison cells became an added visit at meal times for the Orderly Officer – at least Ison still had the privilege of complaining about his food if he wanted to. Not unnaturally, he was not very interested in food, however. He grew thin and seemed to age, I would tell him that it was just intended to teach him a rather grim lesson which I personally thought was in appalling taste. As time went by and pleas for clemency fell on deaf ears however, I became as convinced as Ison himself that the Group Captain really did mean to put him in front of a firing squad. Then one day, when Ison was offering to go on a suicide mission to Germany or anything else rather than have his life wasted for falling asleep, the Group Captain said: 'Right, Mr Ison, you can come out now and resume your normal duties; I think you've learned enough of a lesson.'

In mid-September, Geoffrey Shaw, my squadron commander, offered me deferment of my commission to take up my place at Trinity, Cambridge, returning after my degree and resuming my seniority as of the day I left. I was only eighteen years and six months old, and frankly not showing up very brilliantly as a pilot, so I think they figured out that I was more of an encumbrance than an asset and I might be a better prospect when I was twenty-one. However, I turned the offer down and on 7 October was posted, along with the other four who had been commissioned during the summer, to Peterborough to be trained to fly by the regular air force. Our course was composed of inexperienced Auxiliary Air Force and Volunteer Reserve pilots and a few who had not flown for a long time from the Royal Air Force Reserve of Officers. We were sandwiched between two regular service courses and followed a Fleet Air Arm course of sixty pilots including several marine lieutenants, who were most impressive with their off-duty dress, – blue patrols with red stripes down the trousers and wings on their chests. When I met one of them a year later I heard that the shortage of Fleet Air Arm pilots had been such that they had been on permanent operations ever since they left us, without rest. He himself had been in the sea five times off Norway, Dakar and in the Mediterranean, and there were only five left alive apart from several in mental institutions following prolonged exposure to the sea.

A long, bitterly cold winter dragged our course into five months. I got my wings on 1 December and passed out finally with a summary assessment stating I had had seventy-five hours of flying training and giving a flat 'average' for ability throughout; rather like getting 5 GCSEs and no A levels today.

On the course we were flying Harts and Audax training biplanes with two cockpits, one behind the other. We were paired up for our solo flying, and I got Alex Obolensky, the Russian prince who had made a name for himself before the war as a brilliant International rugby wing three-quarter. We were to train on Harts for dual instruction, Audax for solo flying.

When we were ready to go solo, Alex spun a coin to see which one of us would pilot first. He won and climbed into the pilot's seat. I duly got into the rear cockpit, which was really for gunnery and photographic training, and did not have a seat. One stood the whole time, holding onto the sides.

We taxied out, and then Alex turned into the wind and opened the throttle. The plane bumped along at increasing speed over the grass. Suddenly the floor that I was standing on fell out from under me. I grabbed the sides of the cockpit and yelled to Alex to stop before we became airborne. Not a bit of it! What he thought I was making all the commotion about, I have no idea, but I had to spend the next fifteen minutes with nothing under me, nothing over me, hanging on like grim death whilst Alex put the plane through every horrible contortion he could think of. I later discovered that the bottom that had fallen out was a detachable hatch which could be replaced by a vertical camera when desired.

Alex was in his element. As the acclaimed greatest rugby wing three-quarter there had ever been, and now an air force pilot, he was always being asked to the balls in London, which was only 70 miles away. However, he was upset that at the start of the course he was ordered to take his wings off, as was everybody who already had them, until they were awarded during the course. So when he went to London he put them back on. And each time the *Tatler* and *Spectator* would show Alex dancing with some desirable beauty and sporting his wings. The Station Commander had no sense of humour, and how Alex survived without being thrown off the course I have no idea. His vanity was such that he did not think it sporting to tighten his straps up before take-off, with the result that within a few weeks of finishing the course he overshot the end of the runway in a Hurricane at Martlesham Heath, turned upside down and was killed.

After the course finished, I went on leave and returned to Thornaby a week before my nineteenth birthday. Despite my pleadings, Geoffrey Shaw would not let me have the satisfaction of going on operations before my birthday so that I could brag that I had operated whilst still eighteen. However, he took me as his second pilot on my birthday, after which I became a regular ops. second pilot. The work was boring in the extreme. Flying a few miles off the coast, we would proceed up to Scotland, examining every convoy in detail; much of my job was to write a description of every vessel each time. We would land after several hours, have lunch, take of again and repeat the same performance on the way back. The Ansons stank of leaking petrol and urine, the latter because the 'peeing tube' of coiled metal was invariably over extended and therefore quite useless. All of this made me feel pretty sick when I was not actually flying the aircraft. There was not a German plane, a German submarine or a German mine to be seen – which was really what we were there for. I was therefore not unhappy when the five of us who had gone to Peterborough were posted off again in April, to the School of General Reconnaissance at Thorney Island on the south coast near Portsmouth, to add navigation to our qualifications.

In May 1940 we moved to Guernsey flying up and down the English Channel whilst the Germans broke through the British and French armies and began to approach the coast. On Guernsey, we all acquired various sorts of motor cars. Mine was £10 worth of 1929 Riley Nine, which was fine unless I let it out downhill. Then it would get up to 40 mph but when it reached the bottom it would stop and take considerable coaxing to get started again.

The Germans were on the Cherbourg peninsula and rumour had it that there would be a great attack on our flying field – 'Happy Landings Airport.' The authorities were clever enough to move the red beacon outside St Peter Port harbour to the other end of the island. That night the bombers came and, taking their bearing from the beacon, dumped all their bombs in the sea. On 3 June France capitulated, but for the next three days we continued with our navigation exercises. On the second day we woke to see huge black columns of smoke belching up into the sky out to sea to the north of us. It was two museum-piece French battleships, the *Paris* and the *Calais*, making full speed ahead to go to join in the battle. They looked more as though they ought to have been off to the American War of Independence rather than the Second World War. The captains must have been very gallant men.

We had been awaiting a petrol tanker for some time, and then the news came through that it had been sunk. Unless a relief tanker could get through, the island would be in a mess. The

Station Commander started to round up all the fuel he could find to keep the planes flying. He was even planning to drain the tanks of our cars. On the 6th, we were all gathered together and told we were being evacuated the next day to St Eval in Cornwall. Any aircraft that could not leave would be destroyed. The airfield would be ploughed up and we were to dispose of our cars that evening. However, we were not to tell the local inhabitants as it might cause panic. Of course, the news spread throughout the island before we left the meeting.

Poor Pilot Officer Parrott had that day taken possession of a brand new MG sports car in British racing green, just lowered off the decks of the ferry, and nobody would take it back on board, so all he could do was destroy it. The tide was out that evening and about twenty-five of us drove out to the sands at St Brellards Bay where we had a tank battle to write off our cars. It was stupendous fun but broadsiding or glancing off moving cars on wet sand does not break them, so we all left again and drove down the tiny twisting Guernsey roads to the cliffs in the south. The great thing to do now was to accelerate just around a bend, stop, jump out of the car and hope that the car behind would go into yours. Even that caused little damage so we finished up at the cliffs where, with all the pomp and ceremony we could muster, we ejected the new MG, Pilot Officer Parrott at the helm until the last second, over the cliffs into the sea below. Having followed with all but the worst crocks to get us home, we returned to prepare for our departure.

At daybreak our relief tanker arrived, but, on hearing that we were leaving, the captain decided he was not staying. He could not get back over the harbour bar loaded, so he poured all his precious cargo into the harbour and removed himself at high speed. At midday, a Spitfire squadron flew in with orders to operate from Guernsey. The Station Commander was due to start having the landing strip ploughed up however, so they changed their minds.

Later in the morning, just before the aircraft took off, our orders were all altered as our new accommodation at St Eval had been burned out by an incendiary raid the night before and there was nowhere else for us to go so we went on leave until further notice. I was assigned to the last departing Guernsey cross-channel ferry, the one that had brought poor Polly Parrot's car over, that couldn't leave till 6.00pm because it could not get over the harbour bar before that. Thus, we received a token straffing by the Germans on departure but were luckily left alone thereafter, heading at maximum speed, due west and arriving off the English coast near Falmouth at first light the following morning. We then followed the coast back east to Southampton where we docked alongside a quay filled with an army battalion including field guns, part of an entire motorised division who wanted to know why we were coming back whilst they were just going over to send the Germans back to where they came from. I hope their orders were countermanded, as the Germans took Guernsey with relative ease the following day, capturing an intact 'Happy Landings Airport', with its grass runway untouched and two Ansons that had not started.

A week later we all had to report to Squires Gate, Blackpool, where the School of General Reconnaissance was re-formed. I had a couple of weeks billeted at the Mon Abri pension on Blackpool South Shore, along with three other pilots and four girls on a wakes week from Bradford with their Hudson Terraplane and £400 to spend, on us! After this happy interlude, our course terminated and we all returned to our squadrons.

It was during this time that Lord Haw Haw announced a Nazi edict that when the Germans had beaten the British all our officers were going to be castrated. I often wondered just how much this announcement affected our performance thereafter! I am quite sure it helped us win the war, just a bit!

In July and August, I logged a hundred hours as second pilot on convoy patrol: hot, boring, smelly and very soporific. We saw one U-boat and nearly ran out of petrol searching for a bomber crew down in the sea off the Dogger Bank. 220 Squadron, the regular squadron at Thornaby with us with their Hudsons, were moved further south as back-up for the impending Battle of Britain and we were re-equipped with Blackburn Bothas, which were meant to carry two torpedoes but could not get airborne even with one. The squadron was intended to take over 220's role of patrolling the Skaggerak and Kategat to the north and east of Denmark but had disastrous results because the Botha was powered by two 1,500 hp Taurus engines instead of two 2,500 hp Pegasus ones, for which they had been designed. They were vast, lumbrous machines without much credibility as warplanes. Their huge propeller blades had heavy counter-weights bolted on to their stub ends and these had a habit of flying off. When this happened, the engine vibrated so much it was impossible to keep it going, so the plane had to fly on one engine. This was insufficient to maintain the plane's height except by turning in a complete circle, so it was not much use in making one's way home. Within a month, Bothas were allowed no further than 15 miles off the coast and the squadron had to lie low on its coastal convoy duties throughout the rest of the year. At the end of November, I went as part of a detachment with half a dozen Ansons to Dyce at Aberdeen to relieve better equipped squadrons from coastal convoy duties.

In December, I became permanent second pilot to Hilary Duke Woolley, our squadron commander's brother-in-law, who had been posted to 608, no doubt with a little influence. Hilary had over 1,000 hours of peacetime flying, whereas we all had a mere 400 or so by now, but we still rather begrudged the newcomer's promotion to Aircraft Captain. He did know how to fly though, and I remained with the same crew, amassing about sixty four-to-five-hour stints before the Dyce detachment was withdrawn in the following March. We then returned to Thornaby to be re-equipped with the rest of the squadron with long-nosed Blenheim IVs.

Apart from a few crews being lost over the winter only one other incident marred the period. On 5 March, we had flown up from Dyce to Wick, the furthest aerodrome north in Scotland, and were turning in to land off our left-hand or anti-clockwise circuit. Just as we were beginning to straighten out for our shortish final approach, a Hudson a mile or more further away turned in at the same time as we did and fired a red Very light to signal an emergency approach. Hilary, who was at the controls, saw this and remarked that there was plenty of time and plenty of room on the runway anyway and settled in to put us down as short as possible on the left side of the runway. As we trundled to a stop and were beginning to turn off the runway itself, the Hudson thundered over the top of us with the port engine feathered and the starboard engine opened up for over-shoot procedure, which in itself did not seem very necessary to us. As the Hudson went up again it suddenly took the same left-hand circuit instead of a right-hand one against its live engine.

Hilary said, 'Christ! He's going to kill himself – the fool. Watch him banking, he'll stall as sure as I'm sitting here.' We watched aghast. The Hudson was at about 200 feet in a banked, climbing attitude and as it came back parallel to us a mile or so to the west of the field, its wings came further and further over, its nose lifting. Suddenly, the nose went down and in a slow spiral it hit the ground with a fearful explosion. Shaken to a degree, we taxied to the tarmac, stopped the engines and went to the control tower. Hilary led the way up the steps to be greeted at the door with 'You murderer!' Our luncheon in the mess was not pleasant. Nobody knew where the Hudson had come from or who the crew were, but the looks and subdued comments that were directed at us were all too clear.

It later transpired that the Hudson was carrying our group commander, Air Vice-Marshal Breeze, and the most experienced crew in the whole of 18 Group, captained by a great pilot, Flight Lieutenant Sam Selly from St Lucia Bay, South Africa. The destruction was such that it was not possible to tell who was actually at the controls at the time.

Our scheduled operation that afternoon was to cover a convoy coming through the Pentland Firth, stay with it as long as we could then return to Dyce to land before dark. On the leg back to Dyce, we passed Rathray Head at the south of the Moray Firth and Hilary climbed to about 6,000 feet out to sea, well off the coast, to see better into the setting sun. Suddenly, we met a north-bound convoy and just out of its sight at sea level a JU 88 was shadowing it. An Anson had about half the speed and a quarter the fire power of an 88 but Hilary, still shaken over the crash at Wick, said, 'We'll get him.' Down went the nose, forward went the throttles, up went the speed to about 180 knots. At that moment, the top emergency exit canopy flew off and the cold winter air shot through the cabin like the Arctic blast it was. The rear gunner started trying out his Vickers gun, Hilary fiddled nervously with the gun trigger on the control column and the wireless operator and navigator had each knocked out side windows and attached their 'K' guns to the fuselage structure. At 200 feet the 88 saw us, turned out to sea towards us, opened his engines and passed serenely beneath us before we could get anywhere near. Hilary turned after him, still diving. The 88 thought this was the best thing that had come his way in a long time and I was beginning to think the same. The 88 zigzagged to the north, then to the south to let Hilary's speed slowly close on him. Hilary's face was set white with grim determination. 'For God's sake Hilary,' I said, 'don't you see what they're going to do? We haven't any height left. We're 10 miles out and these buggers are simply going to turn in on us with no trouble at all. For Heaven's sake let's get out of it.' For another agonizing minute Hilary went on, then suddenly, he banked steeply around and headed back to the safety of the convoy's guns. Was I relieved!

CHAPTER TWO

No. 3 School of General Reconnaissance

Through April 1941, I converted to Blenheims. Then half the squadron was posted to the Middle East under the command of one of the flight commanders and I was posted to the School of General Reconnaissance at Squires Gate, Blackpool as a staff pilot and part-time navigation instructor. The school had been equipped with the dreaded Blackburn Bothas and my squadron (608) was the only squadron that had experience of them

We had both Bothas and Blenheims at Squires Gate and I was lucky to find that I was mostly assigned Blenheim duties to begin with. The job was to fly trainee navigators around the Irish Sea on the series of exercises I myself had done the previous year, as a pupil, in the English Channel.

Squires Gate aerodrome is at the southern end of Blackpool's South Shore. The officers were billetted in St Anne's Hotel at St Anne's and the non-commissioned trainee aircrew were under canvas in Blackpool's fairground. There was by now a great intake from the Commonwealth – Canadians, Australians, New Zealanders, South Africans and Indians – as well as Poles and Czechs. The job of Orderly Officer at night at the fairground was quite extraordinary. As soon as lights-out came, up would start the big dipper and most of the helter-skelter machinery. The

NCOs knew a variety of trades and had no difficulty in getting everything to work. The poor Orderly Officer stood on the ground yelling his head off, telling them to come down – and they did not give a damn.

The Air Commodore in charge of Blackpool, who had a beautiful girl, always dressed in purple, his niece we were told, was permanently in residence and whose authority did not seem very good, he was a man of great self-importance. His manner almost provoked the breaking of rules. One of his more permanent problems was Flight Lieutenant Jackson-Smith. Jerker, as he was known, spent much of his time at Squires Gate getting arrested. He had a great capacity for getting into trouble. Having gained one of the first Battle of Britain DFCs on fighter Blenheims over Dunkirk – an immediate award presented to him on his airfield between sorties by the Duke of Gloucester – and having gone on to see almost every member of his squadron shot down before finally being withdrawn for a rest, he did not care for anything that smacked of discipline. He heartily hated the local 'brass', and would tell them so at the least opportunity. Wiry, full of fun, generally a bit untidy, with long streaks of dark hair drooping across his forehead, he was almost always broke or nearly so. He spent all the time he could manage either beer drinking and telling hilarious stories that he enjoyed as much as his audience, or trying to avoid any chance of being mistaken for an asset around the navigation school.

One spot of bother he got into was quite an epic. He had occasion to make a flight to some aerodrome on the east coast. Whether he was really meant to go there or not, I do not know, but he found his old squadron and a lot of pals. He had some poor trainee navigator with him, but he probably did not object to taking several days off his studies on a strange station. A large party was started and just did not stop. The Wing Commander Flying at Squires Gate eventually located Jerker and ordered him back forthwith. At the same time, he realised that Jerker was on the very aerodrome where his own trunk happened to be, not to mention his dog. He suggested that Jerker make himself useful for once in his life and bring them back. Jerker looked at the date and realised he had been away for rather a long time, and decided therefore to set off for Squires Gate immediately.

It was evening and winter. There was snow on the ground and not a lot of daylight left. By the time they reached York, Jerker decided that Squires Gate was bit ambitious that night, and thought he would put down. Neither he nor his pupil navigator were particularly good at map reading over strange country covered in snow in a fast-fading twilight, and they could not find either York or any other aerodrome. Being a fine evening, it looked far lighter to the west than anywhere else, so since that was their general intended direction anyway, they pressed on.

Another half-hour passed, and something suddenly flashed past the plane's wing. It looked like a cable, but that was not possible – they were up at 2,000 feet. Then another similar one appeared directly in front. Jerker missed it with a violent turn. By the time he had managed to avoid a couple more, he realised the horrible truth: he was in the middle of the Liverpool balloon barrage, and the silver thing glinting below was the Mersey estuary!

A few minutes of dodging stout steel cables quickly convinced Jerker that the only safe place to be was down below – and quickly. Spiralling down, he was soon flying just above the water. He pulled back his throttles and got set for a wetting.

The Botha, being of a high-wing construction with a hull rather like a flying boat to look at, took to the water as though it were its natural element. Planing along the top of the water, Jerker decided that it was rather silly to finish up in the middle of the Mersey when he might just as easily take her in nearer the shore, and, accordingly, he opened up the engines and the plane skimmed along happily until he decided where he wanted to stop. Catastrophe came at the last moment. The whole thing had been so easy that Jerker, waiting for the plane to finally settle, had undone his straps. Then they hit a sandbank. Jerker went into the windscreen and was knocked out. The pupil had not been so optimistic and was all right, but the third passenger, the wing commander's dog was killed outright where the bottom of the plane stove in. The wing commander's trunk did not fare very well either.

Late that night, a very wet, bandaged Flight Lieutenant Jackson-Smith reported back to Squires Gate. A not unnatural sequence of events followed: Considerable anger, quite a lot of very nasty words, and Jackson-Smith under close arrest for just about every offence in the book!

A flight lieutenant under close arrest requires another flight lieutenant to keep him company and make sure he stays wherever he is meant to stay – in this case, owing to a lack of the usual facilities, his own room at the St Annes Hotel. 'Boozy' Payne was the first flight lieutenant delegated to this difficult task, but he also ended up under close arrest after driving his Bentley in a fit of exuberance, into the miniature boating pool at the fair-ground a few nights later accompanied by Jerker. That necessitated two more flight lieutenants.

Apart from a grave shortage of flight lieutenants, the authorities had another matter to worry them. Dogs are not allowed to fly in service aircraft, not even wing commander's dogs. The whole affair became quite protracted but the conclusion was certain: all charges were dropped. Indeed I never heard of anybody actually being court martialled there, and probably the RAF had appointed the right air commodore for the job under the circumstances.

Another character was Charles Rose, who arrived at Squires Gate after two brilliant tours on fighter Blenheims. He had eight German planes to his credit, and his hatred of the enemy was such that he could think of nothing other than to kill and kill. His father, an old man who had a small pub in Guernsey, had been taken off to slave labour in Germany, where his back had been broken. Like Jerker, the sole original survivor from his first squadron, Charles had gone on to repeat the performance in his second. During the second tour, he had been operating on the Norwegian coast from the north of Scotland. During his nights off, he used to take a Blenheim unofficially, fly across the North Sea in the dark, then prowl up and down the enemy coastline watching for German lorry convoys on the coastal road, strafe them and fly home again.

Having joined the RAF as a Halton boy, he had been out in India on the north-west frontier before the war as an air gunner sergeant. The CO of his Norwegian strike squadron recommended him for a commission, but, whilst it was coming through, a friend of his failed to return home after a strike. Charles whipped up a scratch crew, took off without the formality of getting permission, and stayed out searching for the lost plane until it was impossible to stay longer. The station commander had given him up for lost when he came back. He came in on his last ounce of fuel and his engines cut out before he had finished his landing run. His commission was cancelled, and was only eventually awarded at the end of his tour.

Charles loathed Squires Gate. To him it was like prison. He did not like people who were reluctant to engage actually with the enemy, and in most training establishments there were one or two of those.

Occasionally, Charles and I went up to London for a day or two. Particularly on the return train journey, he indulged in a most hazardous game. We would be in civilian clothes, and Charles would seek out a carriage with a few troops in it. We would settle down for the journey. After a while, he would get talking to the army boys. 'What are you in uniform for?' he would ask. 'Couldn't you get into a nice reserved occupation like us? You are suckers! We're earning better part of twenty quid a week. Not the army for us – leave that to stupid asses like you!'

It didn't take long for a fight to start. Charles loved a fight. Why we never got thrown out of the moving train, I will never know; I was always certain that was going to be our fate sooner or later, but somehow we always made St Annes station more or less in one piece.

It would have been impossible for Charles Rose to stay at Squires Gate very long, and in early winter he went back to a squadron.

In June, I had had my first flying accident, albeit a little one. I had taken off too soon after the preceding Blenheim and with my undercarriage half retracted, I hit its slipsteam and bounced forcibly down onto the runway bending the port undercarriage leg. We carried out our navigation exercise but at the end I could not get the port wheel down or up and it remained halfway up. I had to make a one-wheel landing. This was quite successful with the unsupported wing only eventually dropping at about 30 mph. Apart from a bent propeller little damage was done. My wireless operator, the two pupils and I were all out in a moment and inspecting the damage when one of the pupils, a turbaned Sikh called P/O Singh, came up to me, embraced me and said what a super landing it was. He then proceeded to open his wallet and produced no less than seven photographs of abominably crashed aircraft which, he explained, were all his own crashed in India. I asked him who the aircraft had belonged to. 'Why, me of course,' was his reply! I suppose that in real life he was a Rajah.

One of the first exercises we did with the pupils was overland at low level to enable them to appreciate the effect of wind drift. This gave us a good opportunity to 'beat up' any friends from the Lake District southward without breaking regulations – at the same time no doubt scaring the living daylights out of the pupils, and sometimes ourselves as well. I bent several aerials on the tops of mansions I knew. One day I had an idea. We had a chute at the back of the Botha through which one could fire a Very light signal. These lights were bright red, yellow, green or blue, or prescribed combinations of these colours. Up in the Dales, at Helwith Bridge near Settle, my grandfather had a big granite quarry. So I flew right into the quarry and fired the Very light down into the middle of it. The fifty men who worked in the quarry were not amused. First, they thought they had been attacked by the Germans, and second, they were scared out of their wits anyway when a huge machine dived into their midst with 3,000 hp at over 200 mph. They fled *en masse* and production was not restored to normal for several days. Thank goodness my grandfather was a wonderfully tolerant man and decided to treat the whole thing as a great joke.

His sense of humour even held up on another occasion. I was taking a Botha back to the Blackburn works at Brough, near Hull, where they were manufactured, to pick up a replacement. I purposely flew over his home to have an aerial look at it on the way over. I saw that there was a big garden party going on – in fact, it was several hundred members of the Leeds Knitting Circle, which my grandmother ran throughout the war, making balaclavas and such like to keep the troops warm. At Brough, I wrote them a letter, put it in an envelope filled with sand, and arranged with my co-pilot to drop it down the chute in the rear of the plane when I gave him the signal. Coming from the east, there was a long rising meadow ending with a ha-ha before the lawn where the ladies, including the Princess Royal, were taking tea at numerous tables. I came up the meadow at low level, lifted over the house and the letter was dropped. I had not calculated that I would take the tablecloth off every single table and that seven of the women would faint outright, and cause every ambulance within miles to come rushing to the scene.

By virtue of automatic promotion I became a flight lieutenant at the beginning of December 1941, and was given No. 3 Flight, which was a Botha flight, which had its dispersal ground in a field on the south side of Squires Gate aerodrome. Right next door was a flight of Defiants which had been posted there for the defence of the Liverpool area against night bombing attacks. Between our dispersal area and the Defiants', was the only piece of covered aircraft accommodation on that side of the field – a so-called 'blister hangar', an arch of corrugated sheets just long and wide enough to squeeze a small aeroplane into, open at both ends, but with tarpaulin curtaining which could be pulled across to keep most of the bad weather out at each end.

The immediate standby Defiant normally stood in the blister hangar, and so it was the night that their T Tommy was called out in a hurry. Returning to base some time later, the pilot got his landing gear jammed half up and half down. Nothing would right it, so he decided to bale out. Flying inland, he gave his gunner his orders and saw him satisfactorily on his way down into the darkness below. Then, flying to the coast, he positioned himself several miles north of the aerodrome, and jumped out just as the plane was crossing out to sea. The wind was blowing from the south-west, and his calculation was to have the wind drift him back to the aerodrome during his descent. Unfortunately, he hit the wing of the plane with an arm as he fell out into the night. Hurt, but not badly, he slowly descended toward Squires Gate.

T Tommy meanwhile was not flying a straight course out into the middle of the Irish Sea as intended. The impact with the pilot's arm had just nudged it off its straight and level course, and it was now making a long, very slow turn, down to the south, back across the coast, and eventually coming north again, descending steadily all the while. It hit the ground a hundred yards short of the blister hangar and somersaulted right into it, whereupon the guns in its power turret let off and blew the whole of the top of the hangar out. The pilot landed a few minutes after, also just yards from the blister hangar!

I soon learned my first lesson about Friday the 13th.

Mechanical trouble was a plague: with Bothas losing counter-weights and clapped out ex-squadron Blenheims losing their engines, the unit had more than its share of fatal accidents and when Friday the 13th came nobody was prepared to fly. The commanding officer was mad as hell so I volunteered, went over to the Blenheim flight and found a couple of pupils and set out to go. The runway was a short one with the 60–70 feet high Starbeck Hotel at the end of it. Just as I became airborne, two-thirds the way down the runway, the starboard engine cut out dead. I jammed the plane back on the runway with full brakes on, burst both tyres and came to a halt a yard off the end of the runway with the Starbeck another 20 feet ahead. I swore not to volunteer for anything again on black Fridays.

It was at Squires Gate that I first encountered a flight lieutenant medical officer called Bamford. We happened to be standing on the tarmac one afternoon watching a Botha returning from an exercise with one engine dead. It passed to the south of the aerodrome then turned to approach into a fairly strong westerly wind. The pilot misjudged and failed to clear the dykes just short of the start of the runway on his approach run. As soon as we saw the crash Bamford asked if I had my car there. I did and in a moment we were racing to the crash scene. When we got there, the plane had been completely crushed. There were compartments for everybody in the plane: the navigators, wireless operators, engineers and so on. Everybody was still in his compartment, but the compartments were all pushed together like a small toast rack. I never had occasion to help at a crashed aircraft again; I doubt if I could have. When a Botha piloted by Pinder Horne of Horne Brothers the clothing traders had its tail cut off by a Polish fighter-squadron pilot and both planes dived into the Blackpool Tower ballroom and station, with horrendous loss of life, Bamford again asked me if I would take him down there. Luckily for me, my car was not available on that occasion.

Squires Gate was so unpopular that we were always volunteering for anything that would get us away from it and I put my name down for an Atlantic convoy as RAF liaison officer. I was not much amused when I found myself assigned to the Destroyer HMS *Winchelsea*, Lieutenant Commander Hawkins, OBE, DSC, commanding, for a south-bound Atlantic convoy – as my next leave!

Winchelsea was an old 'W' Class destroyer which was placed on the starboard flank of a fourteen-strong destroyer screen covering a convoy of about thirty ships, including the *Stirling Castle* with troops on board, a couple of County Class cruisers in the body of the convoy and an 8,000 ton ammunition ship that was made to bring up the rear at a distance.

On the first day out, our ship's refrigeration system failed and thence forward, only condensed milk was available. As I have always detested the smell, I drank my teas and coffees black – very shortly I was certainly the only officer on the ship who was not plagued with incessant sea-sickness.

The convoy went well for three days in rough seas and turbulent weather. A U-boat ambush was beaten off by three of our modern destroyers, who went ahead for them after they had been sighted by the RAF, and two U-boats were sunk. On the fifth day we had to return home along with HMS *Cairo*, one of the cruisers, and *Whitehall*, another 'W' Class, because of our limited fuel range. Before we had disembarked back at Londonderry the news came through that almost half the convoy, including the poor old ammunition ship, had been attacked and sunk the day after we left.

I returned to Squires Gate with the sobering thought of all those Merchant Marine sailors who had to endure the most awful weather conditions and were being slaughtered in their thousands to keep our supply lines operating. I was glad I was in the RAF.

In November, I volunteered for a posting to Singapore and was accepted, only to have the orders countermanded at the last moment. Had I gone, I would have been building the Burma Road for the rest of the war, as that convoy arrived at Singapore at exactly the time it fell and all on board had become prisoners. I also put my name down to become a catapult hurricane pilot on Atlantic convoy duty; I doubt if I would have lived long if I had been chosen.

CHAPTER THREE

1401 Met. Flight

In February 1942 one of our number, who had just married the Blackpool beauty queen, received a posting to No. 1401 Meteorological Flight at Bircham Newton, Norfolk. He was enjoying his new matrimonial state however, and switched places with me, so I went instead. I was certainly luckier than another of our number who applied for romantic sounding 'long-range penetration work'. He ended up on his feet with General Orde Wingate and the Chindits tramping through Burmese jungles for the next several years, riddled with malaria and dysentery.

I arrived at Bircham Newton, 20 miles N.E. of Kings Lynn, in mid-February, in a splendid two-tone green 1 litre MG that my grandfather had bought me to replace the red Ford Prefect. The station had been a permanent peacetime aerodrome, and its buildings were in sharp contrast to the airfield itself: vast, lavish hangars, fine squadron working accommodation, officers', sergeants' and airmen's messes, administrative buildings, married quarters, even squash courts that claimed to possess a ghost from some murder that had taken place in the past, all had been built to last a century. The airfield however, was 950 yards at its longest run, and had a grass surface and a shifting subsoil that could create a pothole overnight big enough to wreck a plane. It was like a piece of Gruyere cheese.

But, what a station! It was the premier operational aerodrome of the Allies for the first two years of the war; more operational sorties were flown from there in that time than from anywhere else. And, what marvellous hosts the north Norfolk farmers were. Norfolk may be the bleakest county in England, but its inhabitants are the opposite.

I reported to the station commander, who was not quite sure what I had come to do – it turned out that 1401 and 1403 Flights were a bit composite. He was very charming however, and sent me off to find my Flight Commander.

The Meteorological flights were not blessed with very good accommodation; there were two big Hudson squadrons based at Bircham, and they had most of what was good. I located our flight offices at the rear of one of the big hangars and reported to the OC, who turned out to be a man I had met at Squires Gate the previous year; Jock Forbes, then a flight lieutenant, now a squadron leader. Second in command was F/Lt Donald Wellings, an ex-bomber pilot, and much to my pleasure, there amongst the other pilots was Charlie Rose, who wasted no time in telling me all there was to know about what went on at Bircham Newton. He lived out with his lovely wife Beryl, whom we used to call Ermintrude, in a flat at Hunstanton. The windows looked out across a narrow road to the back of Hunstanton public swimming pool, offering an enormous and dreary concrete wall to look at, so it was known to one and all as 'Poor View'. Its exterior belied its interior, however, and Poor View gave us all many hours of happiness for as long as we were there.

The work of the Met. Flight was divided into four distinct jobs, each flown on different types of plane. THUM was flown in a Gloucester Gladiator three times each day, and being the proud possessor of the longest record in the RAF, was the unit's pride and joy. T stood for temperature and HUM for humidity. The flight was made to a score or more different levels, accurately reached by use of a barograph placed between the pilot's feet. At each level, the plane would be flown for two minutes at precisely 100 mph keeping exactly to the level. Then the pilot would read off the wet and dry bulb readings on a big thermometer strapped out on the wing struts and record them on a form strapped to his knee, at the same time noting down observations on cloud formation. The top reading would generally be at about 24,000 feet.

This flight had been started in the early 1930s, and had never failed to be carried out, regardless of conditions, for nine years. The flight office was surrounded with framed annual records on its walls, giving each flight and the pilot's name. The cream of the peacetime air force had flown the meteorological flight. Admittedly, in peacetime, there had only been one flight per day; on bank holidays there were no flights and, if there was bad fog, the Air Ministry cancelled the flight. But the record was that they had never failed a flight which was ordered.

When the war started, the great names had gone on to greater deeds, and the Air Ministry had at the same time decided that the wartime air force required three flights per day, with no cancellations.

Now, in the beginning of 1942, the flight still held onto that record; it had never failed in its three flights. A well-known wartime OC was chronicled as having taken off on one particularly foul day, when he had no chance of getting down anywhere in the British Isles. Having completed the climb over base, the Met. Office told him on the radio that the earliest clearances expected would be in Cornwall. He duly flew in that direction, and, when he was near the end of the plane's endurance, he found a tiny hilltop protruding out of the dense cloud which lay over the whole country. He stalled the plane onto it, and landed successfully in 20 yards, just a mile or two from Land's End.

Not for nothing did each plane bear a crest depicting a skull and crossbones under an umbrella, with the motto below: *Semper in excreta*. The College of Heraldry had never approved this, and unfortunately it was ordered to be removed from aircraft when WAAFS (Women's Auxiliary Air Force personnel) were posted to groundcrew duties. The flight was renowned throughout the RAF for its ability to fly even when birds would not, but the real point was that out in the country, away from industrial haze, one could always see at least 50 feet down or 50 yards ahead. The Gladiator, a most versatile plane for the job, with its tail down and dragged along with lots of throttle would respond to any called-for manoeuvre, steep turn or abrupt climb, at 50 mph. There were two ways, one from the north and one from the west, that one could reach Bircham Newton from the sea, with the highest point to cross being the boundary fence.

It was our job to know every tree, every country lane and every building in the way, and then it was not too difficult. The classic, and dramatic, condition was thick fog on the ground. This meant clear air and skies from 50 feet up, so the day would be beautiful and great flying weather. We probably left without being able to see the men on the wing tips who guided us out on the field, and when we came back we simply positioned ourselves by the tops of all the hangars that stood out, fixed our rate of descent, knew exactly the height on the altimeter where we would touch down, and it was our own fault if we bounced. Getting back to the hangars once we were on the ground was frequently more difficult and sometimes impossible. The most difficult condition ever would not be fog, but a 60 mph wind, when eight airmen had to throw themselves onto the leading edge of the lower wing to hold it down long enough to tether the plane to the ground.

Rhombus was a similar flight, but in Blenheims and other aircraft provided for us by Group from time to time. It occurred once a day at daybreak, just off the Norwegian coast. This involved a 200 mile flight over the sea each way at 50 feet.

Prata was also similar, but it was flown with a high-altitude Spitfire, into the stratosphere if it could get there, over the aerodrome like Thum. The Spitfires could get up to 37,000 feet quite easily, but after that it became a painful and tedious job up to about 42,000 feet because one's stomach generally took exception to the extreme unpressurised altitude, and tedious because, when one was making those last few feet, even a slight move in the cockpit to get more comfortable could jog the plane and make it drop 100 feet.

Another idea was under discussion when I arrived, which was to assist Bomber Command by sending a Spitfire over to the continent to take a look at weather there when it was complicated and uncertain. We began this task at the beginning of March. The pilot would broadcast on his VHF radio transmitter, counting from one to ten but stopping at a figure short of ten according to the weather conditions we were looking at. It was repeated every minute, so Bomber Command could receive the information as soon as our transmission came within range. Jock Forbes was the first pilot shot down and killed on Pampa, as it became known, on 15 March.

I nearly did not last much longer. It was 21 March, two days

before my twenty-first birthday, and I was due to make the first
Thum climb of the day. At 6.00 a.m. it was dark, cold, drab and
foggy as I groped my way across from the unit's tiny annexe, by
the Officers' Mess, where our dozen officers had their sleeping
quarters, toward our hangar, outside which I knew would be
waiting my Gladiator, one corporal and two airmen, all three
just as unhappy as me at having to leave a lovely warm bed so
early on such a disgusting day.

As I got closer to the hangar, all sorts of thoughts were going
through my head, including that if Jock Forbes had not been
killed he would already be at the plane, taking this Thum flight
himself, as this was not the weather for someone with little Met.
experience. On a previous flight, when the weather had not been
as bad as this, and which had at least been in the middle of the
day, I had scared myself to death; everybody said how well I
had done, but I knew it had been a fluke. This time I might not
be so lucky. It is one thing going up, but I had to come down
again before the sun had started to lift that dreadful fog. Maybe
I should go and get Donald Wellings, our new Commanding
Officer, out of bed. No, I can't do that, he'll think I am a complete
coward.

As I reached the tarmac a black mass that was the hangar
began to bulge out of the wet slate-grey, and the voice of an
airman unmuffled itself: 'The new chap going up, d'you think?'

'Shouldn't think so, Bert,' came the reply. 'A bit bad for him, I
should say. On the other hand, he didn't do badly the other day.
Ruddy well frightened to death he was, but that's best. It's
blokes that are not frightened when they make a bollocks of
things that really frighten me. Cor, 'ow I'd hate to see our old N
5601 written off.' N 5601 was the Gladiator I was about to fly.

At the sound of my footsteps their conversation stopped, but
what I had heard somehow made me feel a bit better. The men
greeted me with intended joviality and offered me a grimy mug
of char and a fag, the latter despite stringent regulations against
smoking near aircraft. But who cares, at 6.00 a.m. in thick fog? I
gratefully downed the warming mixture of sugar, essence of tea-
leaf and water, equal proportions or nearly so, and almost
accepted the first cigarette of my life, but thought better of that
as I did not want to choke in front of the men.

'About time to put your parachute on and climb in sir,' said the corporal. I had come over from the mess dressed in my flying boots and green overalls, the latter with my old auxiliary squadron badge on it bearing a legend in Latin that was meant to translate into 'By tooth and nail', and I permitted myself for a moment a vision of a completely wrecked Gladiator with me climbing out of it unscathed, clutching my weather report.

Once in the aircraft, I was quickly strapped in, an airman handed me my recording pad to strap to my right thigh, the side of the cockpit was shut up and I started the engine. The last checks followed including in this case the spotlight that I had to rely on to illuminate the huge wet and dry bulb thermometer that was strapped to the struts at the end of the starboard wing and the special barograph mounted on the floor between my legs for giving me more accurate height than the plane's normal altimeter.

Everything was fine, the chocks were removed and the next moment we were moving forward toward the veiled expanse of undulating grass airfield that lay ahead.

At the end of the tarmac, the airmen on each wingtip fell away, gave a half-salute, a friendly wave of reassurance, and then I was all alone. Not quite – up came the voice of the ground radio operator who would guide me back to the airfield in an hour's time. Our transmission and reception were both excellent. After a last-minute compass set and a final engine and instrument check, the all-clear for take off came from the control tower, which was out of sight, but which I knew was only 50 feet to my left.

I slowly opened the throttle, and, as the wheels started to accelerate across the field I glued my eyes to the instruments in front of me. trundle, trundle, bump, and then the wheels quickly detached themselves from the undulating grass which I uncomfortably noticed out of the corner of my eye disappearing in a flash. Now there was just dark murky grey all around. Holding a straight course, we were at 500 feet, the first recording level, in a moment. I throttled right back, kept accurate height and a speed exactly 100 mph. I started the stopwatch and turned the spotlight on to the thermometer on the wing. Thirty seconds, one minute, keeping steady at exactly 500 feet, and 100 mph, and at long last two minutes were up. Now I had to take the wet and dry readings – thirty-six degrees and thirty-four degrees. I climbed to 1,000 feet. It suddenly became lighter as I wrote down the figures, then I burst out into brilliant clear weather at 650 feet. What a lovely day it was going to be, the sun just rising over in the east. I wrote down the height of the top of the cloud. Then I throttled back again.

Back and forth over the aerodrome, gradually climbing higher and higher, every few minutes switching the radio mouthpiece over to 'Transmit' and counting slowly from one to ten so that the radio operator on the station far below could get a bearing on me, then 'Apple Charlie to Brownjack, over to you, over'. Now I switched on to 'receive' and the ground station gave me my bearing. I kept my switch on 'Receive', so that if he wanted to pass me any messages I could hear him. It was now longer between readings as they were taken farther apart the higher I went and the aircraft gradually lost power above 15,000 feet.

Forty minutes had gone since take-off when I reached the top level at 25,000 feet. I estimated that I should be 20 miles east of the station, and called for another bearing. I took a slow turn back toward the aerodrome and then took the last reading. This time there was a difference: the two minutes ticked by as fast as the previous ones had gone slowly. My thoughts turned once more to the 650 feet blanket of fog that lay between me and breakfast. I took one last look around to appreciate one of the most profound and beautiful scenes, a crystal clear view of the pure and tranquil early morning sky stretching into the limitless distance in every direction, with the unbroken quilt of gossamer white cloud far, far, below. Such a sight and the knowledge that unquestionably there can be no other human being sharing it with you, brings a temporary severance from the earth, from all that is evil or petty. The noise and vibration of the aircraft die away, and one becomes part of the outer universe and incredibly contented. Oh, to be able to stay up there permanently, but then that's not possible because the fuel does not last forever. Ones eye looks at the petrol guage and the mind returns to earth, jarringly, to remind one that the last two minutes have gone and now I must return to earth.

I put the stick forward, the nose down and headed for home; up crept the hand of the air-speed indicator and down went the altimeter. 'Apple Charlie calling Brownjack, commenced descent, Vector please,' I radioed. '1 2 3 4 5 6 7 8 9 10 . . . over to you, over.' I switched to 'receive' and waited. Silence. Damn, hurry up down there . . . still no answer. Hell, he hasn't heard me. I tried again. Still no reply. I hoped my set had not gone faulty. No, it was working fine earlier. I tried again, but still no reply. I might have to try to break through without radio help at all, in which case I should figure out where I should be. Calculations based on time, speed and the last few bearings gave me quite a good idea. I should be able to break pretty close to the field and the ground is all reasonably flat for miles. I could double back to the east for a minute or two so as to be sure which side of base I was on, then let down slowly through the fog headed west. All the time these thoughts were going through my mind I went on desperately calling out: 'Apple Charlie to Brownjack, can you hear me?' But there was not so much as the tiniest crackle in response.

I turned west again, by now going at about 90 mph and just skimming the top of the fog. After one last look at everything that had been beautiful, I shifted around in the seat to make myself comfortable, set my teeth and, nose forward, sank carefully forward into the dank, saturated mass beneath.

As I offered up a little prayer, I remembered a standing joke in the unit about a new pilot many years before. No matter what a pilot's previous experience might have been, when he came on to meteorological flying, he had to learn to fly under conditions that he would not have learned how to fly under anywhere else, nor that he would have ever experienced unless he had been caught out badly by a change in the weather and been lucky enough to get away with it. Of course, the greater the experience of the pilot generally the easier the adaptation, but everyone had to some extent, to be 'weened' to a technique new to them. This was done in the only way possible, by putting the pilot up gradually in worse and worse weather.

On this occasion, the pilot had been sent up in conditions which the CO had thought right for him, having regard to the stage he had reached. During the course of the flight the weather worsened rapidly, and, when he had been successfully guided back to the circuit of the aerodrome, the conditions were simply beyond his capacity and there was nowhere that he could fly to where he might land more easily. He had eventually panicked, flying around and across the field, and had started most profusely begging the Almighty to lend him a helping hand. He had long since ceased to ask the ground operator for bearings, as he was at the aerodrome and he could not have made any use of them, even if they had been given to him. However, instead of leaving his radio on 'receive', so as to be able to hear the messages which his anxious colleagues on the ground were frantically endeavouring to pass to him, he had left it on 'transmit'. Thus, for some considerable time, half the station below were treated to a monologue that ran something like this: 'Dear God, if only you will be kind to me just this once, I'll never lie, steal, cheat or be unkind to anybody again. Oh God, I know I'm a stinking louse, a chiseller and occasionally get very drunk and hit my wife, but I'll never do it again if only you'll be good to me and get me on to the ground now and not make me kill myself.'

Naturally enough, despite the danger he was in and the very obvious agony that he was going through, the news spread around the station like wildfire, and before long just about every set on the ground was tuned in to this remarkable conversation with the Deity. Amongst those who were listening enthralled, the story goes, was the Station Commander, and it was just too bad for the unfortunate pilot, when, just before he successfully got the plane on to the ground, he remembered just one more sin, and promised not to repeat last Saturday's performance and try to seduce the Station Commander's beautiful young wife again!

With my switch firmly placed on 'receive' so that history might not repeat itself (not that I had any such potent confession to make – indeed I had met the Station Commander's wife on one occasion so far, and remembered her as a rather frumpy old trout), I cautiously eased my way down through the fog, trying at the same time to bring the aircraft to a height of 50 feet at a time when as near as my rough calculations could ascertain I should be over the aerodrome.

It was now quite a bit lighter in the lower levels of the fog than when I had taken off; something I noted with a great deal of relief. I remembered the rule of thumb that, unless one was flying in the vicinity of a town where smoke and impurities in the air make conditions worse, there would never be a time when visibility would drop lower than either 50 feet down or 50 yards ahead. It was therefore with much hope that I at long last, with great apprehension, eased the altimeter down to 50 feet and looked over the side of the cockpit. Nothing. My heart sank. I must be so near the ground now, yet there was no sign of it. Tall trees could be 50 feet high; so could hangars, and the wireless masts on the station I knew to be 60 feet. I had to follow the rule of thumb, however, and go yet lower. No errors now; the ground was very near, and my stomach was worse than empty.

Forty feet, no ground and I could not see in front yet. Dare I go lower? What option did I have? I wondered where the aerodrome was, but I could not try calling the ground again now; I needed all my attention on what I was doing. Thirty feet. Nothing. Cold beads of sweat began to make me uncomfortable and miserably wet, to add to everything else. Twenty feet, then 10 feet, and then zero – aerodrome level. Still there was dirty grey below me and an opaque grey-white all around. You have to be able to see 50 feet down or fifty yards ahead, I told myself for the twentieth time. But there was nothing else to do but go again. Something had to appear some time. Minus 10, minus 20, minus 50 – this could not be true, I must be dreaming. No, I decided, I really was in this ghastly situation. Then an inspiration struck me – maybe I set the altimeter wrong! How stupid and grossly dangerous. Nevertheless I was much relieved. I checked the barograph to work out my height from that. The altimeter now read just over 100 feet below ground level. I looked down to the barograph on the floor between my legs. My relief melted —— my altimeter was correct.

Then at long last, I saw something indefinite below – not land, not water. I went still lower until I was flying at 150 feet below the height of the aerodrome. Of course, it was a marsh. But where was there a marsh 150 feet below my aerodrome in East Anglia? Then the realisation came to me: I was in the middle of the Wash at low tide. I went on and the mud banks began to turn to fields and I was flying west somewhere in south Lincolnshire. Just then an extra large bank rose in front of me. I just had time to ease the stick back sufficiently to clear it; then, before I knew it had happened, I realised I had crossed a main railway line, over the rails and beneath a blood-chilling array of telegraph wires. This did little to make me feel better but then the railway line gave me a thought. All railways lead to towns, and all towns have aerodromes near them, frequently by the side of the railway lines. So I turned south to follow the railway line, skimming over ploughed fields with my upper port wing about level with the railway embankment. Now I could breathe for a moment. I checked the petrol gauges and the time. I had been in the air for an hour and ten minutes, and had twenty minutes safe flying time ahead of me still. Fine. At one stage I passed over about fifty female potato planters working in a line and wished I was with them.

A little later, catastrophe struck. In Lincolnshire there are supposed to be no oak trees, but there, at almost touching distance in front of me, appeared the most enormous oak tree. With the stick pulled back into my stomach and at full throttle I flew straight through the top. There was a sickening jerk, a horrible rending noise and the sight of the propeller in front all mixed up with flying branches. Then the nose went down and the wheels hit something very solid, maybe the roof of a house. I bounced back into the air and found I was still going, and still following the railway line – but what a mess. The leading edges of the wings were mostly gone and what remained looked like an old crock of a wedding car, streamers of wing fabric flapping everywhere, bits of substructure metal I had never seen before sticking out, and my ailerons and rudder flapping around absolutely useless. And, as I immediately discovered, to maintain any sort of control I now had to fly at 130 mph instead of 80 mph as I had been doing.

I had to decide what was best and I remembered the potato workers, who had been at the bottom of what seemed a lengthy field with the plough running in the right direction. I climbed over the railway and over the telegraph wires, made a tricky, wobbly turn north, and then went back over the railway line again, well past the oak tree, I made quite sure. Then we were heading back on the reciprical track toward the potato field. Now, here are the workers, down I went, cut the engine and hoped. The plane started to settle down before it made contact with earth, then the wheels hit something and I went up and over. The plane came to a rest and everything was suddenly silent. I looked around and saw nothing except, rather quaintly, little strands of tiny, white string coming down from above and quite slowly going down past my chin towards my legs. I watched them for a moment, then grasped that they were marsh gas bubbles. I must be under water upside down. I screwed myself around, dropping my head as low as I could, and found I could just get it out of the water. Now I had to get out. I had slid back the cockpit canopy before landing but that was now jammed firmly closed and I could not budge it. The other option was to prise open the cockpit door panel. There were some locking nuts that held it and I managed to find a penny that fitted their slot. There was the noise of running feet and excited voices. 'Anybody there?' called a voice hopefully.

'Where else do you think I am?' I replied. I wrestled with the locking nuts; eventually they came loose and with a heave I burst the door open, pushed my body through and fell into the dyke. Helping hands assisted me up the bank and a large, buxom farmer's wife said, 'Ee lad, you are looky.'

I looked back at the crumpled up machine that had been a Gladiator. 'Yes,' I replied. 'I certainly am.'

'My son Jimmy near got stoong to death by an adder in that there dyke last year,' explained the farmer's wife.

Escorted by the entire potato planting team, I went to the nearby farmhouse. 'You must have a good, hot bath and some dry clothing,' they instructed.

'Just a moment,' I said. 'I have an important report that I must telephone immediately to my station. Have you a telephone?'

'No, sorry, but there's one a mile away up the road.' An old, heavy iron bicycle without gears was produced and I pedalled off up the road, leaving a trail of dyke water still pouring from my clothes, with my met. readings on the pad still strapped to my right thigh. I got through to Bircham eventually, passed my report on and then asked them to get my flight commander to ring back. Don Wellings was now OC following Jock Forbes' death. 'We were getting worried about you. Glad to hear you're OK. Can you fly her out of there again?'

'You must be joking, come and have a look. I need transport – and the Gladiator, if they want what remains, needs a crane and a transporter.'

I trundled back to the farmhouse on the old bike and they had a hot bath and their son's Sunday best brown suit waiting for me. The brown suit was very welcome but not easy to put on as it was much too small. When I appeared, the whole family were in the only main room, which served as kitchen, dining room and living room. It had a stone floor, big iron kitchen range and about twenty enormous hams hanging from hooks all round the room. Shortly, we went out to look at the crashed machine and I asked if anybody had a camera. It transpired that the son of the local vicar had a Brownie box but only one unused exposure left. He arrived in due course, all of seven years old, and took his picture. 'If you let me have this film, we will develop it at the station and let you have it back in a day or so,' I said.

'Will you let me have a big picture of the plane, sir?' asked the boy.

'Indeed, we will,' I replied.

Whilst we waited for my transport, a huge plate of ham and eggs, more reminiscent of peace than wartime, was placed in front of me. I regret to say that the thought and smell was more than I could take and, instead, the remains of my previous night's dinner disappeared outside the house.

Back at the station, Intelligence took the film and returned the prints less the last exposure, 'The picture of the crash is restricted material,' they explained. 'You can have it yourself but no member of the public may.' What a rotten thing to do! I have always had the thought that I should one day give him a copy of his photograph if I could find him.

The last thing I had done before taking my leave of the cockpit had been to try the radio one last time. Not unsurprisingly there was still no response. Back at the station I found out the truth. Our special frequency was also tied into the mayday distress system. A ship out at sea had radioed for help and my operator had gone to his assistance and forgotten to come back to me. I never asked what anybody had to say to him about it.

Two days later, I was on leave in London for my twenty-first birthday. At my sumptuous birthday dinner I pulled out the picture of the plane and others taken later from the air and my mother's appetite rather vanished.

By the end of June, I had flown seventy Thums, a Rhombus and five Pampas. Flight Sergeant Thimblebee had survived the most extraordinarey crash in a Blenheim returning from a Rhombus in bad weather, only to be killed soon after in Jock Marshall's crew when they were mistakenly attacked by two RAF Whirlwinds at the end of the return flight, off Cromer, their only distinction being that Thimblebee got one of the Whirlwinds with his last burst before they crashed into the sea. The flight's Pampa sorties had been so successful that we were sent second-hand long-range photographic reconnaissance Spitfire VDs and in early June a Mosquito. The Mosquito was brand new and was given the squadron designation J for Jane. The artist who did the Jane cartoon strip for the *Daily Mirror* came down from London and painted Jane coming down in a parachute in streaming skirt and panties, on the nose.

At the end of June, Donald Wellings' wife announced that she was having a child and he requested a posting to more tranquil surroundings. He already had a DFC for a bombing operational tour on Stirlings and was well entitled to a rest. My cousin's husband, Philip Stead, had a problem now. He had been a flight commander in our auxiliary squadron and it was he who had got me into it. Now, he was wing commander in charge of personnel at 18 Group Headquarters and had the responsibility of replacing Wellings. In view of his relationship, it must have been a difficult decision for him to pass the command to me, but I was the only flight lieutenant remaining in the unit. I was only three months past twenty-one, however, and I was informed that I had temporary command until they could find a suitably experienced replacement.

On 29 July, 1401 and 1403 Flights were officially amalgamated into No. 521 Squadron, with me in command as a squadron leader. Charles Rose was promoted to flight lieutenant to fill one flight commander vacancy and Philip Stead from Group told me I should find the other from outside the squadron. 'Anybody you want,' he said. 'And you'd better choose two so that you get one for certain.'

I flew to Peterhead near Fraserburgh on the north-east point of Aberdeenshire and found Philip Cunliffe-Lister, who commanded the Photographic Reconnaissance Conversion Flight, living with his wife Honeybee, in the prettiest little white-washed cottage, with a lovely flower-filled garden. Blister, as he was called, was the son of the Honorary Air Commodore on our auxiliary squadron, Lord Swinton, a former air minister, one of whose claims to immortality had been stepping out of a flying boat in dress clothes straight down 10 feet into the Solent whilst on official duties.

Blister had been in the University Air Squadron before the war and had joined 608 the same day I did. He was a natural pilot and very meticulous. We had gone to the Flying Training School at Peterborough together but he had the hardest luck in the Wings examinations when a helping invigilator looked over his shoulder and corrected an important answer in his navigation paper for him. Poor Blister changed his answer but had been right the first time. He failed the exam and had to retake it. The result was important because the rest of us had as our seniority date 1 December 1939, while Blister had 10 December. We had both then attended the General Reconnaissance School together. In fact, he married Honeybee in Guernsey, and that was funny because the vicar got his hymns muddled and we finished up with 'Lord, dismiss us with thy blessing' which one could hardly call appropriate.

After our return to squadron, Blister managed to get posted to the Photographic Reconnaissance Unit (PRU) at Benson in Oxfordshire, when it was in its earliest days. There he had completed seventy-five operations over the Continent and was now on rest converting future PRU pilots on to Spitfires.

Blister was delighted at the offer of a flight in 521 Squadron so, after a pleasant hour or so on a glorious summer's day in that idyllic scenery of NE Scotland, I was on my way to Squires Gate to rescue Jerker from that dreaded place. He was equally happy. I returned to Bircham Newton, rang Philip Stead to tell him, and a week later both were posted to 521 Squadron to fill the one vacancy. This caused problems and they had to toss for it. Blister won and Jerker was re-posted to 280 Squadron on air/sea rescue on the same station.

As a squadron we now got our own adjutant, Flying Officer Geoffrey Foster, a 50 year-old former Metropolitan Opera Company singer in New York who had been a captain in the Blues in the Great War. He had the most terrific stutter from his singing but was marvellous for me. One day a Canadian NCO asked to see me. He was almost in tears. He explained that he had just found out that his wife back in Canada was having an affair and wanted to know what he should do. I was twenty-one and had not even embarked on an amorous career at all at that stage, whilst he was at least seven years older. I asked him to wait and I went through to the Adjutant's office. 'What the hell do I say to him, Geoff?' With Geoff's help, I learned rapidly. He and I – and I suppose Blister – were the only ones who ever knew my age.

One day I really did let the side down. An airman had accidentally dropped a screwdriver into a Spitfire's petrol tank, and all efforts to retrieve it had failed. When the ground crew announced that the machine was not available for an operational flight, I was furious and instructed 'Sticky' Glue, the flight sergeant in charge of all ground crew, to put the man on a charge. Sticky did not want to, but I insisted. In due course, the airman was marched in. I sat with Geoff Foster and Sticky read out the charge of carelessly dropping a screwdriver down the filler spout into the Spitfire Mk V petrol tank, thereby rendering the aircraft unserviceable. The airman was profuse in his apologies, and I soon became sympathetic. But I could not remember the correct expression, 'You are reprimanded,' and said instead, 'Case dismissed.' Sticky looked daggers at me, it was his authority, not mine, that I had just put an enormous torpedo through!

We also got our own squadron radio officer, an American called Jack Rainey. He was excellent but we lost him to the Americans when they joined the war. We also had our own engineer officer, Flying Officer Buddy Marshal who, along with Sticky Glue, was invaluable when it came to looking after our planes and giving us something we could have reasonable confidence in. Buddy was an old campaigner from the Middle East and needed two bottles of Guinness before he got out of bed in the mornings.

We were moved out of our old cramped accommodation and given one of the permanent D-type hangars, with splendid facilities. One of the first things I asked for in my superb squadron commander's office was an intercom to enable me to talk from the office to any of our aircraft that were flying within radio range. Dignitaries from Group or Command or even parliamentarians, used to come and were most impressed when they were demonstrated to and then were invited to talk to pilots on an ascent at the time. Of course, the pilots used to take the opportunity, particularly in very bad weather conditions, to give a blow-by-blow account that would not have got very far in their official debriefings by Intelligence or met. officers after their flight. But it was very impressive and I managed to get Corporal Leopard, the Radio Engineer, a mention in despatches for his miracle in keeping all those old-fashioned valves in our HF radios working.

When we got our first Mosquito, we also acquired Pilot Officer 'Gert' Green, the brother of an actor who played Sherlock Holmes in films, as our first Mosquito navigator. He thought it would be a good idea to take a camera along. It was a large and cumbersome hand-held affair but in mid-July, when he and I were returning from Rostock in the Baltic, we passed right down the Kiel Canal and Gert lay in the nose and took a line-overlap series of pictures through its whole length. On return, they were sent for analysis. He had found an important camouflaged fuel store on the canal side, which was immediately destroyed. Command immediately ordered all our Pampa aircraft to be equipped with photographic reconnaissance cameras and we started to be given secondary photographic targets. Four more Mosquitos arrived, with four more navigators; Pampa was beginning to be put on the map. We lost aircraft and crews every so often and it was turning out to be dangerous work, as it was almost always done in daylight, frequently with little cloud cover and more often than not it was necessary to go down to low altitudes to measure the height and base of the lowest cloud levels, and then arduously climb all the way back to safer heights many hundreds of miles inside enemy territory.

Another arrival about this time was Flying Officer 'Basher' Bispham. He came from a Hudson squadron in northern Lincolnshire, via a rest in hospital as a result of a particularly unfortunate experience. His squadron's job had been to harass the enemy convoys off the northern Dutch and German coasts; going in low to drop torpedoes and then shoot them up. Basher's chosen target that evening had got the better of the exchange and Basher came out of it with a very badly mauled Hudson on one engine and nobody else alive on board. He was a long way from base and had to fly back into a strong headwind. When he made landfall it was already dark. His radio and navigation lights did not work so he had to land straight ahead on the runway. Unfortunately, German intruders were active and his station had shut off their night landing system. Instead they had lit up the dummy 'Q' site in the marshes a few miles away.

When Basher woke up, he was still sitting in his cockpit seat, 150 yards away from the remainder of his aeroplane, with a sore head.

The enthusiasm for these Pampa flights was incredible. We had a sort of roster ladder. The name at the top of the ladder got the next Pampa, unless he happened to be otherwise engaged or could not be found. In that case the next man took the flight. There were certainly rather nasty incidents from time to time when a pilot took a Pampa because he 'thought' the pilot preceding him on the roster was not available. That was why we developed a reputation for getting a Pampa flight in the air within half an hour of a request for the flight. The pilot or crew who got it did not want the other chap turning up at the last moment and claiming it, and once you were in the air nothing could be done about it.

If we knew about special flights in advance, they were sometimes booked by particular individuals. Basher Bispham (so called because in earlier life he had been a British schools boxing champion) asked specially for the first flight over the Alps. In fact he was over the middle of Norway, doing the Pampa for the famous heavy water raid when the Turin Pampa came in, and Gert Green and I did it instead.

The squadron carpenter made a fine wall case for my office, and it contained maps of Europe for each Pampa pilot and navigator. Our lovely squadron secretary, Corporal Molly Rash, kept it up to date every day plotting the course taken on each Pampa on the individual's own map after each flight.

This all went to create an atmosphere that completely negated our losses, and made a profound impression on our occasional VIP visitors. There were of course many incidents. In August, Blister lost his engine in a Mk V Spitfire just north of Tours, at 34,000 feet in a cloudless sky. Only the day before he had been reading *Tee Emm*, an aircrew magazine that came out monthly and made good reading in the crew room, and had learned that one could glide a Spitfire at 132 mph on the speedometer for its maximum range with a dead engine. He reached Gatwick undamaged, a distance of some 200 miles through hostile skies, without a cloud for cover in sight.

On another occasion he was returning low over the French coast when he saw some strange construction in progress and decided to investigate. It was the first sighting ever of a flying bomb ramp and he was shot up badly circling around it taking pictures. When he got back I had no idea of the importance of what he had found, and gave him hell for badly damaging one of our few long-range Spitfires, and for forgetting that his duty had been to get his weather report back.

Gert Green and I had an amazing escape on one of the Pampas over the Alps. On the outward flight we crossed Switzerland at Geneva and measured the tops of the cloud forming there at 12,000 feet. On the return we were unable to get over the same clouds which were now at about 35,000 feet. Flying at 32,000 feet ourselves we hit the down-current and immediately the altimeter needle started rotating at high speed in the downward direction, losing thousands of feet in no time. The cockpit, which we had thought was reasonably hermetically sealed, filled with fine driven snow. Gert and I, not 2 feet apart, could not see each other, and the windows and all the flying instruments were obliterated. I cut back the engine power as far as possible and the aeroplane was suddenly discharged from the side of the huge cumulonimbus cloud at 10,000 feet; into beautiful sunshine, to our very great relief.

One of our pilots, who had had an appendix operation, went off on a refresher triangular course up the Irish Sea and back in rotten weather. He laid a reciprocal course on his compass by mistake and eventually landed at an aerodrome to find where he was. He had parked and cut his engine before he realised that he was between two Messerschmitts on Brussels Airport! That cost him two years in a prison camp, and us our very first long-range Spitfire AB 131. It had never been the fastest of aeroplanes and Buddy Marshal one day informed me that it had no less than sixteen coats of paint on it, adding several hundred pounds to its weight. We had a lot of aircrew, and the Rhombus crews in particular were hard put to find enough to do, so we decided to strip AB 131 of all its paint. With ten or fifteen men on the job for a couple of weeks and sheer elbow grease it was converted into a silver beauty. Charlie Rose took her up naked and unadorned, without even her marking, to see how fast she could go. Headquarters must have heard about it, for they surreptitiously sent a paint spray wagon over to it when nobody was about. The next thing we knew she was painted bright blue, top and bottom, almost the worse colour for camouflaging purposes. We were so disheartened that we just put the roundels on and that is how the Germans got her.

There was an aftermath to the loss of AB 131. The pilot had recently been commissioned and some time later I received an Air Ministry communication requiring me to state whether the officer in question had acted correctly or through negligence when he was lost. If the latter, he would remain a pilot officer for however long he remained a prisoner of war. Of course, I knew it was his own fault and should have said so. But I was soft and did not. Years after the war I discovered he had become a hero in his own community, many thousands of miles away. In retrospect, did it matter anyway?

One of my first problems when I was given the command was a splendid Belgian, Paul de Jace, a Rhombus pilot with no less than 16,000 hours' flying experience, as he had been a Sabena pilot before the war. He informed me that if he could not fly Pampa flights, at which he would be so much better than the rest of us with his vast experience, he wished to leave the squadron and go elsewhere. I already knew that he had been warned by the Germans that if they caught him flying for the Allies his wife and family would be taken to a concentration camp. Paul said that was irrelevant and I could take it or leave it. I gave in.

A few days later, accompanied by a Sergeant Prag, he was intercepted over Hanover. Prag was killed outright, Paul was mortally wounded and the Mosquito was spinning down from over 28,000 feet. With his last conscious effort Paul got his plane out of the spin and crash landed it on a hillside where he died in the cockpit.

We knew all the details by 4.00 p.m. that afternoon through an agent's report, but the Germans never mentioned it at all, as it was the first Mosquito they had ever captured. There was no mention of Paul de Jace but nine months later Sergeant Prag's body was reported as washed up on Tromsö Island, 2,000 miles to the north, off Norway. We reluctantly decided that airline pilots, used to flying very direct and steady courses, the opposite of what we did all the time, were probably not the best for our type of work.

I was trapped in early September. A Pampa was called for Hamburg in the late afternoon and Command made a rare mistake. An intruder squadron had gone in over northern Holland at 28,500 feet and I had a nearly identical course and height a couple of minutes later. So, over a place called Enkhuisen, I found two FW 190s coming straight towards me. There was no cloud cover and I had been having difficulty with my port undercarriage; the indicator glowed red to indicate that it was not properly retracted. I reckoned that if I simply stuck the nose down with full throttle, it might not do too much good, so I waited for them to close right up, then dived under the right-hand one to split them up. The main thing was to get down to ground level, but 28,500 feet is a long way to go down with a couple of chaps with the latest fighters itching to make a kill. Aerobatically, I was never very good. My rolls were always barrel rolls because when I was upside down, I could never remember which way to push the stick. I reckoned my odds were not good. The FWs took turns in coming at me. I had my navigator, Sergeant Davis, kneeling up on his seat, facing backwards, telling me how far off the next attack was and from which side. We waited until the last moment to turn just before an FW was almost lined fully up on us and we could begin to see the bullets whistling past.

The Mosquito had a peculiarity. When one came in to land, on the last approach to the runway, one opened the radiator cowls to stop overheating on the ground. But simultaneously one had to trim right forward several times on the elevator trimming wheel, as otherwise the nose would go right up. I had figured out, therefore, that if I was in a steep turn and being out-turned, if I opened the radiator cowls I would get more turn – so I did. The result was miraculous! The aircraft flipped upside down, shuddered as though it would fall to pieces and then righted itself 3,000 feet lower with the enemy scarcely to be seen. We repeated this several times, all the time getting further back toward the Dutch coast. With a final sigh of relief we passed over the coast at sea level – and then there was an FW 190 off my port bow, getting ready to come in behind me. 'Watch him Davis,' I said. 'I can't see him. Must be under our tail by now.' We waited but he did not appear. In the sea-level haze he had lost us, or maybe he had no ammunition left. Poor Davis. Every time we had made that turn, he was thrown badly back on to the cockpit floor and half way into the nose bombing position. He was black and blue by the end and although neither of us had realised, he had also vomited all over the place. When we landed, however, we had only one bullet hole in the tail and a chunk of the wing had broken off.

The report went through to de Havillands, the aircraft designers and manufacturers, at Hatfield, where Geoffrey de Havilland himself went up to try to repeat it. He could not and I could understand why: one needed those FWs behind you to get one's heart and soul into it! However, the chief designer Mr Tamblin worked out that that was exactly what should happen. Of course, a week later, it came out as a combat report in *Tee Emm* and other such publications, along with strict instructions: 'In no event attempt this manoeuvre – the aircraft should break in half.'

The postscript to this story is that a few weeks later, Sergeant Davis was posted to a short air gunnery course at the Gunnery School at Sutton Bank. One of the questions in his examination paper at the end of the course was: 'What would you do if you were in a Mosquito and intercepted by enemy fighters at 28,500 feet in a clear sky over Enkhuisen in northern Holland?'

In early October, we lost a Rhombus crew on early-morning take off in bad fog conditions. The captain was Pilot Officer Hank Porter from Milan, Missouri, a 30 year-old American who had been on the squadron flying Rhombus since August. He was a large man with a great heart and a wonderful sense of humour. He had four crew with him, one an unfortunate warrant officer who had only arrived at the squadron the previous evening. There was heavy fog and the control tower would not let them take off until first light, by which time the flare path marking the take-off run was of less assistance. As it was, Hank swung seriously off course on the ground and lifted off to fly straight into the station wireless masts which were 60 feet high. The plane, a Hudson, broke up on the masts and then nosedived straight into the ground at the base of the steel pylons, where an intense conflagration consumed everything that there was.

The families of English members of the crew were notified in the usual way, the letters of condolence were acknowledged and they requested that the remains be returned to them. In the case of Hank Porter, however, it was different. He had left as his next of kin two distant female cousins who lived in London, and these ladies were clearly not interested in taking his remains. They suggested that we bury him locally. So Geoff Foster went down to Bircham village to discuss it with the local vicar. The churchyard was small and all he could offer was a small aviators' corner which already housed two German pilots and Hank had to be placed between them. The funeral was arranged and the cousins, two ladies dressed in black from head to foot, arrived at the station in good time and were escorted by Geoff and me to the graveyard. The funeral detail consisted of eight aircrew and eight ground staff under the command of Sticky Glue. The were to come down by transport from the aerodrome and disembark in a hollow in the road out of sight from the church yard from which they were to emerge at a slow march with the coffin carried by eight of them acting as pall-bearers. Now, there had literally been no remains and some wicked people in the headquarters staff in the station had filled the coffin with wet sand and then loaded it into the transport.

The funeral cortège was late and the group of us at the graveside, including the vicar, waited patiently in the slight drizzle, glancing up the road from time to time to get a sight of the transport coming down the hill. Eventually, it did, at a speed that indicated that Sticky was trying to make up time. Minutes then passed before the pall-bearers appeared, virtually staggering up the 150 yards that still separated us. It was awful, and the two ladies watched with expressionless faces as the cortège came slowly nearer. Eventually they were at the graveside and the coffin was manoeuvered into position over the grave, held by four airmen with two ropes, one at each end. The vicar said a prayer and when he had finished, a bugler from the station blew the Last Post so badly that I had difficulty preventing myself bursting into laughter. Just before he had finished the front rope slipped out of the hands of one of the pall-bearers and the coffin nose-dived into the grave at the feet of the vicar.

I was never so glad to get away from anywhere in my life. As we got into the car to take us back, Geoff told the ladies that a small buffet had been laid on in the Officers' Mess and it was naturally hoped that they would attend before they returned to London. They graciously agreed, and on arriving at the mess they asked to be excused to tidy themselves up. Five minutes later they returned; gone were the veils, gone were the sombre black dresses. Instead, in walked two of the most smashing blondes I had ever seen, dressed in clinging silk dresses with plunging necklines, high heels and silk stockings over the most ravishing legs. The wake turned into a stupendous party.

The girls, it turned out, were in no way related but they had been briefed by Hank to make sure, in the event of his death, that they gave all his flying chums a great time, in return for which he had left them 'all his worldly goods' in his will. God Bless Hank! We unanimously decided he had had exactly the funeral he would have wanted. The girls went back to London the following day – to the best of my knowledge.

CHAPTER FOUR

521 Squadron

In my family there had been a tradition that anybody who did not drink alcohol or smoke before the age of twenty-one would receive the princely reward of £500. Nobody had ever won it, though cousin Basil really did – or should have done – in the Great War. He returned home from the Western Front a captain with an MC and two fingers missing, to celebrate his coming of age. When asked whether he could honestly claim his £500, he admitted that only a week earlier, before a particularly horrific attack over the top to the German lines, the whole battalion had been ordered to take a tot of rum and he had taken his too. 'In that case we can't pay you £500, Basil,' said his grandfather. Basil died of drink very many years later.

In my case, although everybody's generosity had included the finest champagne at my twenty-first, I would not touch it or anything else then, or really until the war was over. I drank ginger beer instead and still did not smoke. In the mess I would quite often spend a few hours talking theology to the padres. Although not a Catholic myself, my experience was that the best padres I had met were. One summer evening when I was talking to the Catholic padre at Bircham, he asked me about my sex life. I told him it was something I had not yet embarked on. He asked me why not, and I told him I had rather bracketed it with not drinking and not smoking. He asked me why again. 'Oh,' I said 'The Bible says you shouldn't in the Ten Commandments.'

'Do you mind repeating them to me,' he asked. So I did. When I got to the bit about adultery, he stopped me and said, 'Is that what you mean? Adultery is sleeping with another man's wife, you know.' I had not ever really thought of that, and when he went on to say that I was in danger of losing my life before enjoying the pleasures of sin, I realised what a mistake I had been making.

The same evening I rang Mary, my girlfriend who lived in London. 'Mary,' I said, 'I'll be down in London on Saturday. Please book us a room at the Park Lane Hotel.' I did not ask her what she wanted, I just told her. The following Saturday, late, we arrived at the Park Lane. I was furious when I found out we had a twin-bedded room, and immediately rang the night manager. 'Put the beds together, you fool,' was his response.

After this I often went down to London and we settled on Bramley Grange, on the river at Bramley near Guildford. My life entered an entirely new phase. Months later, however, we were returning very late, on a moonlit night. Crossing Putney Bridge, Mary said 'stop the car and let's get out, I have something to tell you.' Leaning over the parapet looking down into the moonlit river beneath, she said 'I've never told you but I am married. My husband is a Tommy, serving in north Africa.' I do not think I was heartbroken but I was certainly more than just upset. It was a very long time after that before I saw Mary again. In fact it was to introduce her to Blister, who had returned from prisoner-of-war camp at the end of the war and wanted a date in London, when his own wife, Honeybee, turned out to have become otherwise committed. Blister and Mary married and lived happily together for many years.

As winter approached, we were being called on for more and more Pampas, but crews and aircraft continued to be lost and our major difficulty became providing serviceable, or even available, aircraft in which to fly these sorties. We would apply for replacements, but more often than not an Air Commodore commanding the photographic reconnaissance squadrons at Benson would turn up at Hatfield, walk down the line of completed Mosquitos awaiting delivery and say, 'I'll have that one and that one and that one.' Even the Spitfires were largely second hand; we had what was known as a Mark 1F, with so many old car petrol tanks plumbed into it that one bullet hole would have blown the whole lot to smithereens. An Air Commodore carried somewhat more clout than a mere Squadron Leader, so all we got – if we were lucky – were second hand or rebuilt planes. Sometimes it paid off. In desperation we were sent W 5002, the second Mosquito prototype ever; W 5001 was never allowed on operations I believe. W 5002 was a dandy; it flew far better than any of the others as presumably it had been entirely hand built.

I had my own plane, which I used whenever possible. It was DZ 359, S for sugar in the Squadron; a lovely, graceful machine and my ground crew, under Sergeants Hebron and Treasure, kept it immaculate. I always particularly cared for the throttles which were surmounted by two large ivory-looking knobs, for all the world like big backgammon pieces and I used to wonder how de Havillands afforded this luxury. One day, one of the pilots who had flown S for sugar in place of his own, which was being overhauled, complained that his own plane had a terribly uncomfortable cockpit in comparison, and that he and his navigator had difficulty fitting into it. So I tested it and finding it was true got a tape measure and whereas my cockpit measured 5 ft 2 in across his was 6 inches narrower. This did not seem very fair, so the next time I was on leave in London I rang Harold Balfour, the Under Secretary of State for Air. I used my Father's name, aware that the minister must know him in Parliament for my Father had regrettably remained on Parliamentary duties rather than have taken up his Commission as a General. Balfour was impressed and complimented me on my initiative in coming to him. After that we got just as good service from de Havillands as the PRU air commodore.

It was around this time that the American Eighth Air Force made its appearance, so I telephoned their headquarters, Wide Wings at Hampton Court, and asked if I could go down to see them. I explained our role and pointed out that they would not have a facility such as we could offer them for a long time, particularly as they had no experience of continental European weather and therefore would they like some help from my squadron. They accepted my offer with alacrity and also promised additional support should we need extra planes and crews to deal with their requirements. As it turned out, both Bomber and Coastal Command were very cooperative indeed, and from that time on we were called on to give them the same service we gave our own Bomber Command. In fact, right to the end of the war we were providing the American Eighth Air Force with all their long range met reports and reconnaissance, often up to twice per day, requests coming from 'Pinetrees' as they called it.

At the end of November we had a letter addressed to Air Vice-Marshal Baker, the Air Officer Commanding our Group from no less a person than Air Marshal Saundby, second in command to Bomber Harris, the Head of Bomber Command, commending our work in the most unqualified terms.

> I must let you know how much we value the good work being done by Pampa Flight. Great care and thorough understanding are shown to have been exercised in the observations received, and when height of top or base of cloud was a matter of importance the pilot has invariably descended to make the observation. In addition, take-off within half an hour of the request has become normal practice.

There was a scare at this time and all Mosquitos were grounded because they were subject to a structural failure, called No. 9 bulkhead, which presumably had manifested itself by planes breaking up in the air. I called the whole squadron together and told them about it, and then, to resounding cheers, announced that we would be the only unit in the RAF to carry on flying and would modify them one by one. We got away with it, but if we had not I think I would have been in bad trouble.

I had a shock just before Christmas that brought me down to earth with a thump. I flew a Pampa flight to Munich one morning. It was a beautiful day, I could see for hundreds of miles; the Alps away to the south were in splendid view. Munich lies in a basin with a crescent of lowish mountains to the north and west. I was 50 miles short of these mountains and therefore, still some 100 miles from Munich. It was 12.10 and my view past the mountains was becoming clearer by the minute. There, beyond them was a solid low bank of cloud at below mountain height extending apparently for ever. As the report I was asked for was whether Bomber Command would have visual target sighting, there was no point in going farther; it was much more important to get the information back so that Bomber Command could be stood down. I landed at 2.00 and reported for interrogation. In the middle I received a message from 'Batchy' Carr, the Station Commander, that Bomber Command had requested my arrest pending court martial, for failure to complete the Pampa flight to target and reporting back fake information. My indignant denial was enough to restrain him from actually putting this procedure into operation. A difficult afternoon followed, during which I was suspended from duty. At 6.50 a message suddenly came through that I was cleared.

Naturally, they had to give me an explanation and after being put under constraint of utter secrecy I was told that there were no less than 400 radio operators in Germany who risked their lives transmitting at fixed times visual ground-based weather reports. One time was 12.00 and all reports from Munich area had read clear skies. The next report at 6.00 however confirmed that immediately after noon low cloud had formed into a solid blanket. No wonder Bomber Command did not believe me! I was almost surprised they had not carted me off to jail, in fact, if it hadn't been for Batchy, I think they would have done.

Group Captain Batchy Carr had taken over command of Bircham Newton in the autumn. He was a thoroughly good station commander, tolerant to the right degree and a bit beyond. He seemed to like us and in due course, I think after a serious row with the WAAF officers, he kicked them out of their super married quarters and gave this splendid detached house to 521 Squadron as our own Squadron mess. In all fairness, we were the only unit small enough to fit into it; but it was quite a privilege. We got it with a caution, however. 'Braithwaite, if and when you decide to have a party there you will invite me. I will tolerate no abuse and no nonsense.'

We moved in in great style. My batman, Wally Coe, in peace-time a milkman from Desbrough, who always wore a flat hat rather than a forage cap because it was more like his milkman's hat, and carpet slippers because he had flat feet, organised our care and life entered quite a new phase. I was able to bring my Labrador puppy, naturally called Pampa, onto the station and half a dozen Rhode Island red chickens so we had plenty of fresh eggs even when Batchy stormed into the main mess one evening shouting, 'Who has been after my bloody ducks?' In the stony silence that followed, Pampa walked in with feathers sticking out of his mouth in all directions. Nevertheless, all that happened was that Pampa was ordered off the station, permanently.

In January, I was sent on one of those unaccountable courses that came up from time to time – a gas course of all things, in the middle of Salisbury Plain. 'Somebody has to go, chum,' said the Station Adjutant. 'This time it's you.' I had to have an inoculation in the arm, which made it ache, so I decided to let Lou Kelly, our junior pilot and a schoolmaster in peacetime who I think may have been better at school-mastering, fly me down in our new Miles Master, the training aircraft which we had recently received for conversion training of pilots on to Spitfires.

The Master has front and rear cockpits with a canopy framework over each which opened separately for entry and exit for each of the two pilots. Both had a full set of controls but flying visibility was much better from the front cockpit. So Kelly went in front and I got in behind with a parachute bag full of my kit on my knees. It was so bulky that I could not even reach the control column. It also made it quite difficult for Lou to pull his control column back very far as it synchronised with the one in the back cockpit and my bag was in the way.

We set off in fair weather. I balanced a map on the top of my parachute bag as I was slightly uncertain of Lou's navigational abilities. The route took us over Benson in Oxfordshire and then over hills about 1,000 feet higher with only the Andover valley crossing the route at 400 feet lower altitude. There was a dog-leg route to the south-west from Benson which would link up with the Andover valley at the lower level and, as cloud base was already down to 1,000 feet at Benson, I was surprised when Lou went straight on. Being a new aircraft I was not very happy that our intercom did not work, so that I had to shout to Lou to suggest he turn around and take the alternative route. But with the noise of the engine and with his helmet tight on, he interpreted my shouts as encouragement. Since we were flying at about 20 feet and farm houses whizzing past, it would have been dangerous to seize the controls even if I could have done so with a bulky parachute bag in front of me. Anyway, aviation law

Squadron Leader Denys Braithwaite, DFC★.

The officers of No 608 (North Riding) Squadron Royal Auxiliary Air Force seen here in April 1941 standing in front of a Bristol Blenheim Mk IV. From left to right, Flying Officer Sammy Fenwick, the Author – at that time a Flying Officer, Squadron Leader Philip Stead, Wing Commander Geoffrey Shaw, DFC, Squadron Leader Clay, Flight Lieutenant James Woolcock and Flight Lieutenant Peter Vaux.

The Author's first prang. The Blenheim was landed on only one main wheel on 5 June 1941 with this result.

The 'Met' squadron badge. It was not officially approved.

The Duke of Kent inspects the Met Flight two days before he was killed in a tragic accident whilst flying in a Short Sunderland over Scotland and on his way to encourage British servicemen in Iceland.

The Author and a Gloster Gladiator Mk II.

The result of a Thum (Temperature and Humidity) flight made on 21 March 1942 in a Gladiator. The Author took off in thick fog and climbed to 24,000 feet when radio contact was lost.

In an attempt to land and with only fifty yards visibility the aircraft struck a tree and a house. When making a force-landing it struck a dyke junction and somersaulted into the dyke.

The first photograph of the de Havilland Mosquito when it was released from the Secret List during 1942

A reconnaissance photograph showing the beaches of Dunkirk and their defences taken in April 1943.

Taken with a vertical exposure from 23,000 feet, this photograph shows the Italian end of the Mont Cenis Tunnel in autumn 1942.

had it that Lou was captain of the aircraft. So I sat there following his route with a pencil, drawing our exact route. I suddenly saw that we were heading straight for a hilltop marked at over 1,100 feet. Nothing I could do could communicate this to Kelly and, sure enough, the ground suddenly rose sharply. Lou yanked the nose up and we had hit the hill with force, then bounced back into the air again.

I pulled the emergency release for my canopy and it came away in my hand, leaving the canopy in place – I was trapped. I buried my face in the parachute and waited for the inevitable nasty return to earth. But it did not happen. I looked up, and we were climbing, the propeller apparently undamaged. There was a splash of red on the port window, and Lou yelled that he could not fly it any more. I had instinctively set my stopwatch, and I now broke the steel bowden cable that held my safety harness and somehow managed to stuff my parachute bag behind me, all the while trying to fly the aeroplane and maintain direction and speed. I levelled out, did a quick calculation for the Andover valley, which was only one minute's flying speed wide and started a descent. Lou was not keen, but I managed to persuade him to stay in the aeroplane. At an agonizing 600 feet I broke cloud right in the middle of the valley, turned west for Andover aerodrome and reached it after a few minutes.

I flew around on the circuit two or three times, nose up, nose down, jinking, and jerking to try to get the wheels down. They would not budge. So I told Lou that as he was in the front seat he should belly land her. Another petrifying minute passed while despite my yells to put throttle on, he headed into the airfield's grass basin at a horribly low approach speed. This was silly with a damaged plane that might stall well above its normal stalling speed. But it did not and we made a lovely flat belly landing in soft ground. I was never so glad to be back on the good earth in one piece. When we got out, I looked at Lou to see where the blood had come from. There was none – being a training aircraft the Master had a dab of red on the port cockpit window and green on the starboard!

I despatched Lou back to Bircham Newton by train, telling him that he would probably be feeding my chickens for the next two months and that he was to say nothing untoward until I returned, only that we had had to make a belly landing owing to undercarriage failure. And then I found transport to take me to an unpleasant four days of lectures on the techniques of gas warfare, interspersed with periods of lying in the middle of Salisbury Plain under a groundsheet being pelted with mustard gas bombs.

Two great friends of my family were Ronnie and Betty Gilbey of the Gilbey wine and spirit firm. At my twenty-first birthday party Ronnie had told me that if ever we wanted supplies for a squadron party he would be glad to provide them. With great generosity, a case of gin and a case of whisky had arrived some time before and were lying under my bed intact. Shortly after my return from the gas course, somebody arranged an evening hockey match between the WAAFS and 521 Squadron. In January there is not much daylight in the evening, so the hockey balls soon became invisible and we retired to the mess, where I broke open the cases. This developed into an impromptu party, with everybody enjoying themselves until the early hours.

The following morning I received a summons to the Station Commander's office. 'Sit down, Braithwaite,' said Batchy. He opened the drawer of his desk and pulled out what looked like a piece of Venetian lace. As he held it up I could see it was my writing on the remains of a letter. 'What the hell are you doing writing letters containing classified information? Don't you know mail to Northern Ireland goes through the censor?' I had written a lengthy letter to one of our ex-pilots who had been posted to the Met. flight at Aldergrove outside Belfast, telling him who was still with us, who was not and what had happened to them. I also mentioned the latest marks of planes, with four-bladed propellers and so on, with which we were now being re-equipped. The censor had gone through it with his scissors like a dose of salts. Indeed, it was very hard even to make out the continuity from what was left. 'Bloody fool, be more careful in future and think what you are doing before you do it!'

I thought that was it, but then out came another piece of paper. It was the crash report from Andover. 'Kelly's crash landing from undercarriage failure,' he quoted from my report on the incident. 'What the bloody hell is half a moor's worth of heather doing stuck up inside the belly of the aircraft? There is no heather on RAF aerodromes.'

I had to confess the whole truth, and Batchy listened sternly with folded arms. 'Right, as for Kelly, he's for prunes.' Then, after, a pause, 'But, that's not all.' He rang the bell on his desk and in came his secretary, Corporal Molly Rash, looking red-eyed and jaded. 'Corporal, will you kindly confirm in front of Squadron Leader Braithwaite where you were last night and why you arrived for work an hour and a half late this morning?'

Poor Molly, to whom I was much attracted myself, stammered out how the party had started and what time it broke up.

'You may go, Corporal,' said Batchy, and Molly, saluting as smartly as she could with tears pouring down her cheeks retreated to the door and fled, no doubt to have an unrestrained weep at her own desk.

'Braithwaite, I told you I was to be invited to any party you had in the mess without exception. You have broken the rule and you and your squadron must pay for it. You have further caused me inconvenience and been responsible for my personal secretary not only arriving late, but in a useless condition and dreadful appearance.' Batchy paused, then went on. 'The corporal knows the rules as well as you and I have already told her that I shall have her replaced. That is entirely your fault and should be on your conscience. As for you, you will all be moved back into the station mess today.' Finally, after another pause. 'Three serious breaches of regulation and discipline in one day amaze me Braithwaite, and I haven't forgotten your bloody dog either. The next time you step out of line in any way whatsoever, you will lose your squadron and return to being a flight lieutenant for the duration.'

'Yes, sir,' I eventually said. 'I know I deserve everything you have said, but may I ask you not to be so hard on Corporal Rash; it was my fault and not hers.'

'I sympathise Braithwaite, but I shall not change my mind. She will go.'

'She is an excellent secretary, sir, and it would be an awful pity for Bircham to lose her. I know it will be a bit of a down-grade, but we have applied for a new secretary in 521. May we have her?'

Batchy looked at me, sucked his lips and paused, and I thought he was about to let off a rocket that would impel me halfway across the station. Then: 'All right, one mess lost, one pilot off to prunes and one new secretary gained. Think yourself

God Almighty lucky. You may go, but don't ever again have to come back here with a load of sheer stupidity, disloyalty and nonsense as this morning. There will be no further chances.'

I saluted and left. Pity the mess, I thought, pity poor old Lou Kelly with the horrible months ahead squarebashing on Brighton front under the most foul and objectionable warrant officers the RAF can find, but what a win. Molly Rash was to be my private secretary!

As it turned out, I lost two pilots, not one, that month to Prunes Purgatory as it was called. Sergeant Clayton, one of our Spitfire Prata and Pampa pilots, came in to land and went through the steel direction-finding mast on the side of the aerodrome. He made a mess of the Spitfire and Batchy, who had a habit of taking over from squadron commanders when he felt sufficiently angry, sent for him. Clayton was a stocky, well-built man with a darkish face and black hair. He looked like a coal miner, not the sort of person you would want to meet in a fight after closing hours. Batchy gave him fourteen days' jankers. Clayton had applied to live off the station in Bircham village with his wife some time before. When someone went down to the village to pick up his toilet things for his time behind bars, they discovered that Clayton's 'wife' was not his wife at all. It turned out that she was still up north and not even receiving marriage allowance; Clayton was simply enjoying life with his latest girlfriend. Jankers was therefore followed by a month at Prunes.

Clayton had his own special, and most unimaginative, method of getting away from interceptions. He would simply put his Spitfire into a 20,000 feet vertical dive. I did it once by mistake in thick cloud and getting it out required all the strength I had in my body. When Clayton was killed near Lille the following November, I heard that he made the most terrible hole in the ground, so I supposed he had tried it once too often.

Poor Wally Coe, our batman, thought he was going to lose his wife as well. When we checked out of the married quarters, he got two weeks' leave and went off to Desborough, where his wife Florence lived. As Wally put it when he came back, he had been observing what some of his young officers got up to, so he thought he ought to impart some of this astonishing new knowledge to Florence, to whom he had been married for fifteen years.

In short, he made love to her. At the finish, Florence turned to him and asked, 'Are you going to divorce me now, Wally?' Such must have been life in Desborough but then come to think of it, a milkman presumably goes to bed very early in order to start his round at 4.00am, so maybe it isn't so surprising!

In early March, 1943, I was in the Operations Room being briefed for a Pampa into the area of the Heligoland Bight when one of the very pretty WAAF intelligence officers came up to me, thrust a signal into my hands and said, 'You're not meant to see this till tomorrow, but I thought you would like to, in case you don't get back.' Gert Green and I had both been awarded DFCs.

A week later, a press photographer came up from London for a day and a night, taking pictures of all the aircrew with our aircraft, eating their pre-operational bacon and eggs and so on. Shortly afterwards I got a call from Group who said they were considering whether to allow publication of the squadron's activities. I said it would be excellent for morale. In the end, however, they refused on the grounds that it would make our work more difficult as they did not think the Germans paid too much attention to us and they did not want to draw attention to our activities. After the war, it was confirmed that in fact, they put an average of two interceptions against every sortie we ever made. This made sense considering that Bomber Command waited for our reports before the final decision as to whether to go or not, even to the point of bringing six or seven hundred aircraft that were already making their climbs to altitude on their initial triangular courses over England back to their bases if our report warranted it.

When I received a copy of the *Yorkshire Post*, with my name and picture printed with the citation beneath saying that I had made many daring flights over England and the North Sea, I did think that Group were stretching the security aspect a bit far.

The squadron operations record book reads for 5 March.

12.55 Mosquito Pampa by Pilot Officer Hatton with Flight Sergeant Bartolotti Navigator to Aachen and Osnabruch. After reaching Aachen, descended to measure cloud base and on climb back starboard engine overheated, so remained at 24,000 feet. Accurate flack in Osnabrück region and evasive action caused further overheating. Flying back at reduced speed at 7,000 feet was bounced by two Focke Wolf 190s. Aircraft was hit and immediately burst into flames. At 4,000 feet observer baled out followed by pilot, landing in sea two to four miles (6 km) apart, approximate position 30 miles (50 km) out from Yarmouth. Pilot was picked up by RNML 25 two hours later. Observer missing believed drowned.

This short narrative by no means tells the whole story. The 'Wing Commander', as we called George Hatton because he had flown on one side or the other in the Spanish Civil War had a small bristly moustache, and his Pilot Officers' stripe entirely belied his manner. He had come back across the North Sea fairly slowly and at an unusual height. Two crafty and lucky enemy pilots had stuck themselves in at a distance behind him and his blip on the coastal radar station apparently obscured theirs. He and Bartolotti were obviously not watching out and were badly shot up before they realised anything was happening at all. George became as angry as a hornet and entered into a dogfight with them with his burning plane, trying to ram them with it, for want of a better weapon. The German pilots apparently did not think this particularly amusing, so they got out of the way, fully aware that they had made their kill anyway. While all of this was going on, George had told Bart to bale out and he himself did not go until his own clothes were beginning to burn. Having maydayed his problems for the last time, George got out in due course and parachuted into the sea, his dinghy inflated instantly and his clothes scarcely had time to get wet before he was in it. The Mosquito had crashed in the sea while he was coming down and the German pilots dived over him, waggled their wings and went home. I and another Mosquito from the squadron were rapidly on the scene to find them and guide the navy in to pick them up. Of Bartolotti or his dinghy, there was no sign. He was a strong swimmer and the sea was calm so his disappearance was puzzling but nobody ever knew what happened. George had seen him splash into the sea safely. The only possible explanation we could think of was that by a million to one chance, the plane had actually crashed on him.

A couple of weeks later, George received a letter from the Murray Parachute Company.

Dear Pilot Officer Hatton

We understand that you have recently saved your life by means of one of our parachutes. We are most proud of this, but with great regret have to tell you that because you used one of our parachutes you do not qualify to be a member of the famous Caterpillar Club, nor receive the coveted Caterpillar Insignia, as this is exclusively connected with the Irvine Parachute Company.

However, we do wish you to have a suitable memento in recognition of your feat and under separate cover you will shortly receive from us our substitute for the more fancied insignia.

Yours respectfully

Murray Parachute Company

By post the next day, George received a parcel containing a most superb silver Georgian tankard with his name and details of the incident all engraved on it. That afternoon, the Parachute Section was besieged by aircrew from every squadron on the station asking to change from Irvine to Murray parachutes.

Towards the end of March, I received an order to go to Pathfinder HQ at Huntingdon, the office of Air Commodore Bennett, together with Blister. Donald Bennett was a thinish, energetic man. He had an reputation as one of the best navigators in the world and was the pilot of the Mao composite piggy-back flying boat with which he had tried to reach Cape Town non-stop before the war. He had started the war as a flight lieutenant and had reached stardom when Churchill selected him to form the Pathfinder Force in order to co-ordinate the efforts of Bomber Command to deliver their bombs on their prescribed targets rather than largely into useless countryside as had hitherto been the case.

Bennett had an engaging personality and he explained to Blister and me that the Pampa flight was to be transferred into his command on 1 April and that he would like both of us to come with it. It would come as 1409 Flight to Oakington near Cambridge and would there become a squadron again, with due promotion for both Blister and myself. It did mean starting our operational tours all over again, but the thought of joining the rather glamorous Pathfinders and the promotion that went with it was a very fair inducement. We both accepted and drove back to Bircham Newton to carve up the squadron and move to Oakington. 'Press on,' said Bennett as we left. That was his stock phrase.

It was difficult to divide the squadron up. Almost everybody was keen to leave Coastal Command, which was very much the workhorse command, without the glamour or press coverage, and go to where their exploits received constant publicity and where, for every medal given in Coastal, virtually dozens were awarded. The ground crew were similarly motivated, I tried to get them all together to arouse the same fervour that was generated at the time of the No. 9 bulkhead crisis, but it flopped because the half who knew they had to stay behind were almost in tears. At least one man virtually was, and to my dying day I shall remember telling one corporal, a fine rigger named North, that his greatest talent was organising squadron parties and that there would be no time for that where we were going. I can still see the poor fellow's face.

We took eight Mosquitoes and eight pilot and observer crews and ground staff headed by Flight Sergeant Glue, and Sergeants Hebron, Treasure and Henry, a total complement of about seventy personnel. The last entry in the squadron operations record book was touching.

> This was a sad day in the Met. Squadron for it was the last day 521 Squadron functioned as such. Today, the Squadron was split into two flights, 1409 and 1401. 1409 Flight comprising Mosquitoes only with Squadron Leader Braithwaite in command, departed for Oakington and Bomber Command, 1401 flight remaining at Bircham Newton to do Thums, Pratas and Rhombus with Gladiators, Spitfires and Hampdens under the command of Flight Lieutenant Bispham. Thus ends the history of 521 Squadron – the little Squadron with the big reputation.

This was not quite the total carve up. Charlie Rose and Buddy Marshal, the Engineering Officer, left for Prestwick to take part in the formation of the Mosquito counterpart squadron to the dam-buster Lancasters, their ultimate job being to skip their bombs over the submarine nets at Trondheim Fiord and sink the Tirpitz. In fact, they had terrible trouble with the spinning bombs, which rotated out sideways through the wooden structure, leaving a great gaping hole in the side of the Mosquito. Eventually, Wing Commander Tait and his Lancasters beat them to it with conventional bombs, a raid which Tait not only led, delivering the lethal blow himself, but which he followed up by circling the battleship for the rest of the attack to draw enemy fire on himself. He was presumed to be in line for a VC for this, but as he had not even one bullet hole in his Lancaster, and one had to have sustained damage from the enemy to receive the VC, they had to give him a further DSO to add to the four he already had.

As for Charlie Rose, he was itching to get back to where he could damage the enemy properly, and not simply send back weather reports. In 521, he had even propounded the idea of us going with all our Mosquitoes and dropping bombs into the base of the Lorelei, that great rock that hangs over a bend in the river Rhine, and is a special symbol of German patriotism. He reckoned that with well-placed bombs we could roll it off its perch and drop it into the bend of the river, blocking navigation most successfully whilst Hitler worked out what to do about it. On one Pampa I went to have a look at it and decided that the less we said to higher authority the better. But Charlie was quite happy to settle for the *Tirpitz*, and so was Buddy so long as Turnbury could still produce supplies of Guinness for his early morning sustenance.

Basher Bispham had been a splendid Pampa pilot, but he had to stay behind as he was the only remaining flight lieutenant. One small story about him. One day when we did not have any serviceable twin-engined aircraft for the next morning's Rhombus, I set him down to do the flight in a long-range Spitfire. Whilst it was the best we could find, this particular machine had an engine that had a habit of cutting out periodically and starting up again about thirty seconds later. Basher came into my office, drew himself up to his full height of about 5 ft 8 in saluted, and said gravely, 'Sir, do you realise you are sending me to my death?'

'Even if I am, Flight Lieutenant Bispham,' I replied, 'Get the hell on with it and come and apologise when you return.' He did! For all that, 600 nautical miles of flying at 50 feet over the North Sea, half of it in the dark, in an unarmed aircraft with a single engine which had a habit of stopping periodically, was a bit tricky. Basher survived the war.

On 1 April, whilst we flew the eight Mosquitoes to Oakington, Sticky Glue and his men set off in eight transport lorries, bulging with all our equipment, even including atop one lorry my chicken coops and twelve Rhode Island reds. The coops had opened or fallen off *en route* and when a red-faced Sticky arrived at Oakington two hours late it transpired that all fifty or sixty airmen had spread out over the fens to recapture our precious hens. Half of them had fallen into ditches and all were covered in mud from head to foot.

Unit personnel medical records had to go with the commanding officer for delivery to the new station HQ. I thought I would check ours and there to my astonishment I found my own. Nobody was supposed to see their own medical record and so mine should not have been included. When I had been at the School of General Reconnaissance in Guernsey in early 1940, I had suffered an eye injury when the big boot of a pilot who later was the first to capture a German submarine from ther air hit my open right eye as I sunbathed on the sands. It was painful and for some time caused me considerable impaired vision. Thus, it was no surprise when I was ordered to Group HQ at Petrevie Castle in Scotland to have my eyes properly examined. There I had been ushered into a small waiting room where I was left for a couple of hours. Now reading my record, I discovered that they had made spyholes through the wall and had actually been testing me for sleeping sickness! Geoffrey Shaw, my old 608 Squadron commander, had noted that on the long boring, hot smelly Anson trips, if I was in the navigator's position behind the pilot I would go to sleep! At Petrevie, I gathered I had done the same, 'but the case is not serious and such is the shortage of pilots you'd better see if you can fly him out of it', the report summed up!

Oakington, outside Cambridge, was another world, an eye-opener. Apart from ourselves, there was only one squadron there. No. 7 Pathfinder Squadron flying Stirlings, who could put up twenty aircraft on their best night. There was a Group Captain CO, two Wing Commander flight commanders, and twenty-seven squadron leaders. When we walked into the mess, it was full of mostly youngish men with more medals on them than we had ever seen, DSO, DFC and DFM together were almost commonplace. We comprised sixteen aircrew, with just Gert and me sporting DFC ribbons, which suddenly felt absolutely minuscule. Added to that, they also wore the Pathfinder insignia, the gold-coloured metal albatross, at the top of their pocket below the ribbons. What I also did not know then was that Bennett had made a deal with the authorities, that, as his Pathfinders were going to take enormous losses, every Officer got a one rank promotion automatically when they earned their Pathfinder badge.

The operations room was a worthy counterpart. We thought we had a pretty good set-up at Bircham, but here were a bunch of girls that all looked as though they were straight out of Hollywood, and they acted with a smartness and efficiency that suggested that they had been trained for it their entire lives.

We all had rooms in the main mess. I shared with Blister, which was a mistake because he had brought his saluki dog, Kavama, with him. And, when I was not there, Kavama, a great big aristocratic Persian beast, would appropriate my bed. When I wanted it back, he would stare at me, for all the world telling me to go and lie down on the floor myself. If I hit or pushed him, he would disappear at great speed and Blister would be furious as he would never get it back in under several hours.

Now that Bomber Command had the Pampa flight within itself, to do what it wanted with, rather than in Coastal where there was slightly more reticence when 'asking' for flights, the work increased. The better summer weather was coming and the raids could be more frequent. Moreover, Bomber Command was becoming ever larger. I was still flying with Gert, but as he became Flight Navigator as well, he was not always available. So I did my last flights in April with Bob Taylor, a pilot officer observer who had joined us in early March.

Bob was a big broad man, almost too large to fly observer in the rather cramped navigator's seat. He was from Bolton and uncle to Elizabeth Taylor. He had trained for a sea career, but in 1929 the slump arrived and he found himself the sole breadwinner for the family, so took work as a speed cop. He was an exceptionally nice and kindly spoken man.

Towards the end of April, Bennett gave us the bad news that the Treasury had vetoed the elevation of the unit to squadron, or rather independent status. This meant that Blister's and my promised promotions were cancelled. A dilemma also raised its ugly head in the form of a signal from the Air Commodore SASO at Coastal HQ addressed to me at Bircham Newton. It ordered me to proceed forthwith to take up an appointment as Chief Flying Instructor at No. 9 Operational Training Unit for photographic reconnaissance crew, at Dyce. It ignored the fact that I had been a month in the Pathfinder Force and out of Coastal Command, and also that I knew absolutely nothing about teaching people to fly.

I went to see Donald Bennett. 'Don't worry, I'll sort it out,' he said. Then, after an hour, he called me. 'I can't!'

I went back to see him. 'Will you let me go and talk to them myself, sir?' I asked.

'Certainly, and better than that you will go with my driver in my staff car and represent me.'

I arrived at High Wycombe and it was not long before a very youthful wing commander, a wingless wonder, who looked as though he had not started shaving yet, ushered me into the air commodore's office.

I had decided beforehand that a reassuring historical account of the matter, emphasising that I had been with Pampa from its inception and was now loath to leave it, would probably make the Air Commodore more amenable. It did not. 'The unit has left Coastal with a flight commander and a squadron commander, but it is now only a flight. We are fed up here with experienced personnel being filched from us by Bomber Command.'

'But sir, I am promised promotion to wing commander and I can not get such promotion or responsibility in the appointment you have given me. In fact, I do not know anything about teaching people to fly.'

I was interrupted abruptly. 'This war is not being fought for the benefit of individuals, Squadron Leader! If you do not shut up and get out of here, you will arrive at Dyce as a flight lieutenant!'

I made one more try. 'But sir, Air Commodore Bennett told me to say that I came here representing him, on his authority. I can't just go back and tell him I am now under your orders and pack my bag. So far as I know, I am still under Bomber Command, not Coastal.'

'Fuck that little bumped up flight lieutenant! Who the bloody hell does he think he is? Get out of here and my last words to you are: 'Go to Dyce without further delay otherwise you will regret it for a long long time.'

A couple of hours later, I was back in Huntingdon at Pathfinder HQ and Bennett saw me immediately. I told him word for word what had been said. When I had finished giving him the other air commodore's description of him, Bennett's face twisted with anger. 'Right,' he said. Beside his desk was a veritable display of telephones in various colours. He seized one and to my astonishment said, 'Give me the Prime Minister.' He was not there so Bennett picked up the next phone. 'Get me Lord Portal.' Portal was the Chief of the Air Staff and I was rapidly beginning to wonder what shape I was going to emerge in after this lot. Whilst he was waiting, he looked up at me and said, 'I think you had better get back to Oakington, Braithwaite. Carry on normally until I speak to you again.' I rose, saluted and left the office, wondering what on earth was going to happen.

At the beginning of May, I was in the Operations Room being briefed for a Pampa to Karlsruhe with Bob Taylor when I was called to the phone to speak to Bennett. 'Afraid I've lost the battle for you, Braithwaite. You'll have to go, but don't worry, let it die down a bit and I'll have you back in a few months if you want to come.' That was it. Group Captain Fresson, the Station Commander was in the Operations Room and suggested that I detail a substitute as pilot. 'I'll get skinned after all this if you go off on the op. and don't return,' he said. I talked him out of it however, and off Bob and I went.

When we were climbing short of the Belgian coastline, the engine superchargers, which should have cut in at about 15,000 feet, failed to do so and no coaxing could persuade them to change their mind. So, with only about half power, I radioed back that we were returning to base. The cloud cover appeared to increase a bit as we went in and we managed to get up to just short of 30,000 feet, nose up, tail down, dragging along at 130 mph. It was not very healthy, but Bob could at least look straight back over the top of the tail, which was an advantage, and if we dodged from one cloud bank to another so as to stay in close proximity to them, we should be able to dive out of trouble if any came. What I did not know was that, moments after I had radioed my return, two interceptions on us had come on the screen back at Control HQ and then we had vanished. We had actually flown out of range, but Fresson was more than agitated, because he thought the heavens were going to come down on him for letting me go. I landed some three hours later and I think he sat down and wrote a citation for a Bar to my DFC out of sheer relief.

CHAPTER FIVE

No. 9 OTU – Dyce

Group Captain Colquhoun, the Station Commander at Dyce, was suspiciously pleasant when I reported. 'Well Braithwaite, it's nice to see you back in Coastal. Those bomber boys, you know. Glad to have you back and I am sure you will enjoy being here and do a good job.'

'Thank you very much sir,' I said. 'I am sorry there has been all this commotion, but the main problem is that I don't quite see what I can do here. I can't teach people to fly, I have never been an instructor, and I am pretty certain I am temperamentally quite unfitted for it. The thought of letting somebody else who can't fly properly fly me completely unnerves me.'

'That's all right, Braithwaite, you will be doing more of an executive job anyway, and I have given you the Spitfire flight, where there is no dual instruction.'

That seemed fine, and I was much relieved – until a few days later when I was posted to Babdown, a Wiltshire aerodrome, to learn to become a twin-engined instructor.

I was a most unwilling pupil, having to learn the endless patter that an instructor has to speel out to his protoge about flight, night flying, one-engined landings, forced landings etc. I hated and resented it and at the finish gave my instructor my elder brother's battle dress as a bribe, elder brother not needing it any longer as, having come over initially in the Canadian Air Force, he had now transferred to the US Army Air Corps. The

Bribe was for my assessment which was to read 'Flying Instructor – failed'. But it did not work and I got above average as a pilot and average as Instructor. I was given Category Q, multi-engined, but I never found out what that meant. I returned to Dyce in the middle of August.

I now had to run the Mosquito conversion flight. After a week with only one fatal accident, there was a mess party and the following day the whole station appeared to have hangovers. By 11.00 not a single aircraft had taken to the air and the Wing Commander rang in a fury and told me to get something airborne in a hurry. I went into the pupils' room, found a new flight sergeant and told him I would take him up on a familiarisation flight, which meant that I was flying, not he. After one or two take-offs and landings, I said I would show him the stall characteristics of the plane. Climbing to about 5,000 feet over the Grampians, I slowed right down and pulled the nose back. Sure enough, the nose and starboard wing dropped down and we went into a right-hand spin. I had never done this before in a Mosquito so, after a couple of spirals, I applied left rudder and hard right engine to bring it out. The result was a flick and I found myself in a sharp left-hand spin. It had reacted exactly like a single-engined fighter. It now needed a lot of port engine accelerating us downward. We were rapidly running out of altitude, as the Grampians are high, and we just pulled out with a few feet to spare. I returned to land.

The flight sergeant said nothing, but shot straight off to the Wing Commander's office to request reassignment to Spitfires. He had had enough. Not long after, I was in the Station Commander's office. 'Squadron Leader, the SASO Coastal Command warned me that I would have trouble with you. You completely unnerved one of our most promising pupils and nearly killed both of you through sheer carelessness. I am reporting the incident to Command and you may expect disciplinary action to follow.' That was 22 August. That evening I rang Pathfinder HQ and told Bennett I was for the high jump. 'For God's sake get me out of here,' I said. 'Ah,' said Bennett, 'It so happens I have 139 Squadron available and you can have it if you would like.'

'Thank you very much, sir.'

'Sit tight and I will deal with everything.' Two days later, my posting to 139 (Jamaica) Squadron, No. 8 (Pathfinder) Group, Bomber Command, came through. I had few goodbyes to say and on the 27th, in a US Air Force Piper Cub piloted by my brother, I arrived at Wyton to take up my new appointment. Operational flying was more conducive to the happy life than training establishments, I decided.

Several things had happened since I had left for my brief return to Coastal Command. I had taken up an invitation by Jack Rowland Robinson, the MP for Blackpool South and Adjutant to the Eagle Squadron, to give an address to the American Eighth Air Force HQ at Wide Wings at Hampton Court when the 8th Air Force had come over, I had approached their Commanding Officer, General Eakers to offer our meteorological services, similarly to our work for Bomber Command. I explained that, logically, they did not know European weather and had no unit of their own that could do it for them. This was gratefully accepted and I had a promise of support for an enlargement of 521 Squadron to cater to their needs.

Jack asked me to show him my address and was somewhat disconcerted when I told him I was going to ad lib. The performance in their war room started at 11.00 every morning and consisted of a series of well-trained intelligence officers coming on one after another, with a big map behind them of the area of the war they were covering, and then rattling off their reports in precise, meticulously clear terms at the highest possible speed.

When I was ushered into the auditorium to hear the last two reports before my address, I realised that the fireside chat approach with lots of Anglo-American co-operation that I had intended, was out of place here. Unfortunately, only a couple of days before, the Americans had accused one of our Pampa flights of not doing their job properly. In all of Pampa's history we had an unblemished record and it appeared that it was the Americans who had boobed, not us, and somebody at their end was trying to foist the blame on us.

I started off with a brief and clearly boring account of how all our routine flights operated. Then I got on to Pampa and, instead of giving them the guff about the Anglo-American relationship, I launched straight into the incident of two days before, I might even have suggested that they did their own meteorological reconnaissance in the future if ours was not good enough for them.

At the end of the session, Jack Rowland Robinson, clearly disconcerted, brought General Eakers over to meet me. He offered me a pointedly weak handshake, and then asked if we would care for any decorations for the excellent work we were doing. I told him that the US DFCs which corresponded to the British DFCs would be most appreciated. Jack Rowland Robinson was never quite the same with me again, but a US DFC did arrive at Oakington a week or two later, for the Commanding Officer of the Met. Flight. I had left, Blister had been lost and a grateful George Hatton received it as manna from heaven, to add to his Georgian silver goblet.

I had arranged the Wide Wings address to coincide with my visit to Buckingham Palace, to receive my DFC from the Monarch. So the next day I found myself in the anteroom that overlooked the spacious lawns and lake. There must have been three of four hundred officers of all services, due to receive the same level of medal: the DSC for the navy, the MC for the army and the DFC for the air force. We milled around for hours, rather like cattle, I thought, waiting in stalls on auction day.

The leading recipients on this day were the Dam Busters, with Guy Gibson at the head, to be invested by the Queen with the Victoria Cross. Her Majesty had never had this duty to perform before, but the King was in North Africa. In fact, it was the first investiture by a queen since Queen Victoria and Her Majesty was enjoying it tremendously, and spoke to everybody about their exciting experiences, with no thought of the time.

Thus it was many an hour before I eventually arrived in the Investiture Room. Ahead of me I could see the dais with a sloping ramp up to it, and at its bottom, the most formidable character I had ever seen. Gilbert and Sullivan were scarcely in it. Allowing for the plumes that sprouted out of his black cockade, he was all of 8 feet in height. He had a wickedly hooked nose and the great sword that was attached by a 12 inch wide scarlet sash and belt that must have been all of 5 feet long.

When eventually it was my turn next I stood by this huge personage and he spoke. 'We are already an hour and a half late for lunch. There are two hundred of you still to go. You will advance up the ramp, turn left at the top, take six smart paces forward, not pushing Her Majesty off the dais, you understand. There you will stop and salute smartly, then wait to be spoken to. Whatever Her Majesty says to you, you will reply, "No, your Majesty". Remember we are hungry and I am watching you.'

Just then, with a flick of his great sword at my ankles, I was sent on my way. I turned left, went six paces forward, came to attention and saluted. There in front of me was one of the most beautiful women I had ever seen, who was actually looking at me. Her eyes glowed, and she asked 'Where are you stationed now, young man?'

'At Dyce, ma'am, near Aberdeen.'

'Oh, my dear, how lovely. Do you know that is so close to my home, Balmoral. Do you know the Dee valley?'

'Well, ma'am, I do fly down it some times at the end of a trip, and it really is quite beautiful.'

'Oh, indeed it is,' replied Her Majesty, and with that went into a five-minute travelogue on the Dee valley and its surroundings. I did not really take too much of it in, as I could feel the man at the foot of the dais staring at me every moment I was there. I only thanked God at the end that the exit ramp off the dais went in the other direction and I never had to see him again.

After I had left 1409 Flight, Bob Taylor had started to fly with Flight Sergeant Durrant, an old campaigner who had originally been a Rhombus pilot. On 14 June, they were caught unawares in north-west France at 28,000 feet near a place called St Pierre la Riviere, about 30 miles east of Le Mans, by enemy fighters which crippled their aircraft in the first attack. Durrant immediately told Bob to get his parachute, which unlike the pilot's which was attached to his backside and sat on, was stowed in the nose of the aircraft with elastic clips. Durrant simultaneously jettisoned the escape hatch canopy above their heads and unfastened his straps. On the next attack, the whole tail was cut off and as the plane nosed down into a vertical dive Durrant was ejected straight out.

Bob had still not got his parachute, but had managed to release it. He was now lying pinned to the floor by the centrifugal force generated by the tight spin in which the stricken plane was descending. For agonising minutes he tried to reach his parachute, which was rotating in the nose, with the spin. Eventually, he got hold of it and with a superhuman effort, attached it to the clips on his harness webbing on his chest. But he still could not raise himself off the floor to reach the exit. Down and down went the plane until suddenly at about 2,000 feet the whole Perspex nose broke away and Bob literally threw himself through the hole, pulling the parachute ripcord at the same time. His parachute had barely opened when he hit the ground heavily within a hundred yards or so of the aircraft, which naturally exploded.

Bob dragged himself to his feet and disengaged the parachute whilst looking round to see where he was. He was in a field not many yards from a road bounded by hedges. Almost immediately, a man emerged from behind a hedge, rushed over, collected the parachute up as fast as he could and, beckoning Bob to follow him, ran off down the road. Coming to a house, he literally pushed Bob through a door and disappeared.

Shortly, another man appeared and asked Bob in broken English if he was hurt. On being told he was not, he told him to follow him over some fields. Soon Bob was under a tiled shelter and alone again. And from there, for the better part of half an hour, he watched Durrant descending on his parachute in the middle of that cloudless summer afternoon.

The Germans were waiting for Durrant when he landed, but they had not seen Bob's parachute open, it had been so low. When they arrived at the scene of the crash, to find an aircraft dug deep into the ground and burning fiercely, they did not even try to discover if the navigator was still there.

In the evening, a couple of French people came back, picked up Bob and took him to a barn belonging to a largish farmhouse. Presently the lady of the house brought out food and wine, a razor, a bowl and soap and water. Bob rejected everything that might implicate them in harbouring a British serviceman. He sent her back with all the utensils and settled down to make his temporary home in the hay, ensuring as far as possible that if the Germans did find him, to all appearances it would seem that the farmer had never known he was there.

He waited six days and nights, with food brought out periodically by the farmer's wife. They made it look as though he had scavenged vegetables and even a chicken. He did not shave.

Each night he noticed that at about 11.00p.m. a large flight of

German transports went over, headed for Brest. He had his escape compass under one of his tunic buttons, a product of Blister's teaching; Blister had always been a keen potential escapee, with maps, compasses, money, sewing gear etc., stowed in every conceivable place over his body and uniform

Now, Bob felt he had some vital information to relay. He knew the Germans' times and their direction. They were always meticulous in their routine, a great weakness of theirs in the wrong circumstances in war time. There had been a time when Coastal Command had tracked their great Condors, heavily armed mammoths from Norway, around Ireland, down to France and then back again the next day. Noting their exact timing, a squadron of Beaufighters had been positioned to intercept them north of the Shetlands and shot down five of them in succession before the Germans realised what was happening.

Bob made the farmers understand that he must speak with the local Resistance and a man came shortly who could speak English. Bob explained the message he wished to be transmitted to London. Shortly after Bob had left the farm, during his Resistance-accompanied hazardous train journey to Paris most of the German transports were eliminated in one night.

The journey to Paris was fraught with danger as Bob could speak no French or German. He was dressed as a peasant, had forged identity papers describing him as a deaf and dumb labourer imported from Latvia to the dockyards in Brest and going to Paris on orders for medical attention. His papers were scrutinised and his clothing and small valise searched several times at various check points, but he managed to remain passive throughout, albeit extremely scared. He eventually arrived at the Gare d'Austerlitz, where his guide left him. He was now on his own.

From there he was quickly swallowed up in the anonymity of the Paris Metro system and headed for the next destination provided by his last guide. He later learned that the escape pipeline system through Brittany and Normandy had been infiltrated and largely destroyed only a few days before his arrival, so the Resistance fighters themselves had had to find ways to get him away, rather than using the well-oiled escape machinery that would normally have handled him. They had only been

able to go so far, and Bob had now arrived there, just a small
street with a few shops; a dead end for him – no names, no
addresses, just the small street.

It was 11.00 on a fine day with the sun shining down on the
new leaves of the plane trees that grew out of the grids in
the sidewalks. A few went about their daily business. Bob
walked the length of the street, then back again on the other side
looking and smelling like a tramp, with a heavy growth of
stubble over his face. He was examining the contents of the shop
windows, as much to appear normal as to see what was inside.
And then, suddenly, he saw it – a small notice which shouted
out to him. And he knew, the instant he saw it, that there was
not a living German who would understand its significance.

He opened the shop door and walked in. There was only a
woman behind the counter and Bob turned to examine the bric-
à-brac for a few moments whilst he made certain in his own
mind. The woman spoke to him stiffly in French. Bob turned and
said, 'I am an escaping English airman.'

There was a pause, then she asked in a slightly lower voice,
'Your name, monsieur?'

'Pilot Officer Taylor,' he replied.

'Come into the back Mr Taylor, please,' she said in good
English.

In the room behind was an untidy bureau littered with paper,
broken objects brought in for repair or discarded and now
forgotten, and an old cat washing itself on a low stool.

'Do you have any identity Mr Taylor?' the woman asked,

Bob stooped, unlaced his right boot of the pair provided for
him by the Resistance, peeled off his dirty sock, and extracted
from between his toes, an RAF tunic button which he unscrewed
to show his escape kit compass. He laid these on the bureau
together with his forged papers, then took off his hat and pulled
back his unkempt hair, between which, and his eight-day
growth of beard he showed his right earlobe, savagely torn away
from the surrounding skin and still dangling badly as a result of
his dive through the nose of the plane without disconnecting the
intercom from his helmet.

'That is sufficient, Mr Taylor. I do not need to know more. I
had hoped you would arrive. No more talk please. You will hide
in that cupboard.' Here she indicated a low, triangular door

under the staircase, with old cartons piled indiscriminately in front of it. 'Here is a cup of water and a cheese roll from my lunch, which I will replace. At three, I can close the shop and will bring back your courier this evening.'

Bob squeezed himself into the small space with the water and the cheese roll, pocketing the papers as well as his compass button. Soon he fell asleep.

At about 6.00, he'd already woken when he heard voices and the cartons being moved. The door opened and a young girl beckoned him to get out, which he did with relief and considerable pain from spending so long in his cramped position.

The girl did not speak English, so the woman told him. 'You will be taken by Louise – this is not her name of course, but it is the one you will use if necessary – on the Metro. You must not know where you are going so you will be blindfolded. Louise is your distant cousin. You are still the Latvian deaf mute in Paris to see the medical people and she is putting you up for the night as you went to her home this morning and fell heavily, hitting your head badly on the railings outside the house – which is why your head has to be so heavily bandaged. Do you understand this completely clearly Mr Taylor or, as I should say now, Herr Johann Groupe?'

'I understand perfectly, madame and thank you,' replied Bob. His injured ear was bathed and cleaned and then made to bleed freely afresh. A gauze pad was applied and then his head was bound up with bandages torn from an underskirt and finally, adjusted to appear as though it had slipped so that it was now covering his eyes. Louise then led him out of a door which he knew was not the one he had originally entered.

Louise guided him as fast as condition would allow to what he deduced was the Metro from which he had emerged that morning. She bought tickets and they boarded a train. After six stops, they alighted and went up an escalator to another platform. The train arrived, they boarded again and set off. Bob counted the stops and, at the sixteenth, they disembarked.

Leaving the Metro they were once again on a pavement. They walked for 290 paces, turning to the right after 100 and to the left after a further thirty. Then there was a knock at a door on street level and Bob was guided inside. A female hand took his arm, no words were spoken and he found himself being assisted up two flights of stairs into a room and finally, sat on the side of a bed. The bandage was carefully removed, and he found himself in a small bedroom, frugally furnished, looking at a tidily dressed woman in her mid-thirties. Of Louise, there was no more sign.

'Pilot Officer Taylor, I am Alexis and I shall be looking after you for a short time, I hope, whilst arrangements are concluded for your return to England. The view out of this window is, I regret, drab, as you say, consisting only of a blank wall on the other side of the street. Nevertheless, I must ask you to keep the window shut at all times and never to appear before it. If you should be discovered here, it would not only be me who would be shot. All these streets are under perpetual observation from the Germans and informers. I pray you to be most careful, and patient. The patience is also very important.'

She left and in due course brought Bob a somewhat meagre plate of bread, potatoes and some sausage meat that did not taste much like sausage. 'The food is not good, not very much, but they know what I eat in the local shops and how much I have to spend.' She added, with a ghost of a twinkle, 'I think you may be big enough to survive the short time here.' She went downstairs and returned with two tiny glasses of red wine. Giving Bob one, she lifted the other. 'May you bomb the dirty bastards out of this country and I hope, out of this world when you get back home, Pilot Officer.'

The narrative ends here. Bob never told me how he returned to England from that safe house, nor what the mysterious sign was that no living German would recognise, nor is he alive today to say. After the war though, he went to Paris and by studious study of the Paris Metro maps and many journeys of sixteen stations, he did eventually find Alexis to thank her. He also returned to Normandy where, to his great distress, he found that five Frenchmen had been shot for aiding his escape. Today there is a plaque in the village of St Pierre la Riviere placed there by Bob and Durrant after the war in memory of these five brave Frenchmen and women. Robert and Marie Ferdane, Georges Mandrin, Alexandre Martineau and Robert Yvon.

Bob had been fully briefed by the French before being returned to England, and the official record of his debriefing says that after several locals had taken the parachute and the

Mae West he had walked to a small village 8 miles away in four hours and early the following morning had been invited into a house where, between that and a barn, he had been kept in reasonable comfort until his escape could be organised. This was said in order to cover up what really happened, but alas to no avail.

Those brave people of St Pierre la Riviere were of course complete amateurs, whose natural instincts had been to help this British aviator who landed in their midst. They were virtually condemned to death the moment Bob landed in their midst. The Germans naturally came and enquired of the navigator after picking up Durrant. Everybody denied seeing him. Once the embers of the burnt out plane had become cold enough to be examined they found out immediately that there was no second body inside. So, they must find him. A Monsieur Prevot, a civil servant from Paris, arrived to spend a holiday in the Normandy countryside, choosing to stay at the *Auberge* at St Pierre la Riviere. He was a jolly fellow and they remember now that he also happened to speak English. He did not have to wait too long for Georges Mandrin, who liked his wine, to let the cat out of the bag. The next day Prevot and Robert Yvon, the owner of the *Auberge*, went to Paris, probably on the pretext that if with Yvon's help they could catch up with Bob, they would all be let off. Yvon was never heard of again, and the following day the farmer and his wife, and Georges Mandrin and Alexandre Martineau, were arrested by the Gestapo, and, according to the villagers, who really could not have known for sure, taken to Auschwitz. The Resistance shot Prevot when the Germans had gone.

Bob's return to England was cloaked in as much secrecy as his departure from France. He probably left by Lysander from a secluded field in a remote part of north-eastern France. However, it was extraordinary how soon the grapevine knew that he was back. He suddenly turned up at the Met. Flight at Oakington on 16 July, still sworn to secrecy for some strange reason, as it might as well have been published in the newspapers. As soon as I got my posting back to Pathfinders, I rang Philip Hazleman, who had been Philip Stead's gunner in the old auxiliary squadron at the start of the war. He was now a Wing Commander in the Air Crew Postings Directorate in the Air

Ministry. In terms of the utmost secrecy, but asking me how on earth I had got wind of it, he confirmed that Bob Taylor was now back in the UK undergoing debriefing. But if he wanted to come to us, he would arrange it.

The third thing that had happened in my absence was that we had lost Blister. He had assumed command on my departure, receiving the DSO that I had recommended him for just before leaving. I had found out that it was customary in Bomber Command for anybody achieving 100 operations whatever his previous gallantry medals, to receive the DSO. I had gone to Group HQ, uncertain whether his operations in Coastal Command would count towards a Bomber Command medal. The SASO had bawled me out, as if it was my fault that Blister had not already been well decorated. Bomber and Coastal Commands saw medals in entirely different ways; they were imbued with different mentalities. As for me, however, I would never have begrudged the heavy bomber boys anything anybody thought to give them; it was all too often graveyard flowers in advance.

Blister had been having dizzy fits which were diagnosed by the station Medical Officer as being a result of spending too long flying at high altitude. He was ordered to stop flying operations for a couple of weeks, and took a rather overdue leave along with his navigator, Sergeant Johnny Boyle, a lovely little chap with great guts and determination.

On the night his leave was over, Blister came back to camp to find that there was nobody reasonably available for a night-time Pinetrees Pampa called for 'as soonest possible'. All the crews had been flying non-stop. Blister said he would go, but Johnny Boyle had not yet arrived back. He found a fairly new observer, recently arrived and ordered him to the Operations Room for briefing while he organised the plane. He therefore only met him in the cockpit just before they started the engines.

They had a long triangular course to fly over western Europe and at daybreak were reducing height to come back to land at Oakington when, to his horror, Blister suddenly recognised the rooftops of Stuttgart 300 feet beneath him, remembering them from his PRU days. Their navigation had been wrong, he had little fuel left and they were still 60 miles inside the German/French border.

Flying west until the petrol gauges read almost empty, Blister crash-landed in a remote tree-lined valley in the Black Forest, in an area that looked very uninhabited. They got out of the plane, removed everything they needed and that they did not want the Germans to get and then set fire to the plane. Once the fire was going successfully they made for the woods on the side of the valley and started to walk towards France.

That evening German troops arrived and began searching through the woods just as soon as they realised that the crew were trying to escape on foot. The troops spread out, line abreast, 5 yards apart, with fixed bayonets with which they prodded every heap of leaves or heavy undergrowth. Both fugitives were hidden under piles of leaves, both had bayonets within inches of their bodies and both were lucky to be missed when their piles were raked with casual rifle fire. By a miracle, they remained undetected for two days whilst the Germans made two more similar beats through the woods. Blister even had a healthy kick on his left shin from one of the Germans, who luckily took it to be a lump of wood.

Eventually, the Germans gave up and Blister and his navigator were able to start making their way through the last 20 miles to the border. As they approached it however, they saw that the fields they had to go through had more and more skull-and-cross-bone warnings around them, indicating that they were minefields. At the last habitation before the border, they decided to risk going through the village itself, and there they were trapped and arrested.

Captured RAF officers in the Ruhr area were always interrogated by a detestable intelligence officer known as Creeping Jesus. Blister was marched into his presence after he had been thoroughly searched and had two sets of maps of Europe and copious magnetic buttons and other aids taken from him.

He was complimented sarcastically on his escapology preparations which he was told were a waste of time. Creeping Jesus then proceeded to tell Blister everything about our work, about the people of ours they had in POW camps and of course, about Blister himself and his father, the late Air Minister. It was all so convincing that Blister almost came to the conclusion that we had had a permanent ongoing active informer within our own ranks. In due course he arrived at Stalag Luft 111, to be greeted by nine of our number who were already there. In due course he became officer in charge of map production as he was the only one to arrive in the camp with a full set of maps, his third, which he pasted to the sole of one of his feet and was never found by the Germans.

CHAPTER SIX

139 Squadron

I had some mechanical trouble with my MG on the journey south from Aberdeen, but at last limped it into a garage I used in London. The following morning my brother, who was by now a captain in the US Army Air Corps volunteered to fly me up to Wyton, by Huntingdon, my new aerodrome, in a small US intercommunications plane. After a bumpy ride in an aircraft I decided was constructed of papier mâché and string, we arrived at Wyton and I said a relieved 'thank you' to my brother and set off to find the 139 Squadron offices.

When I arrived there, I found the Adjutant's office empty. The next door said 'CO', so I went in. There, sitting at the desk was a group captain wearing DSO and DFC ribbons. 'Sir,' I said, 'what are you doing here?' This is my new squadron and I think this is to be my office.'

'Oh, you're Braithwaite, are you?' Said the group captain. 'What has taken you so long to get here?'

'How long do you think it takes to pack up from one station in the middle of Scotland and drive to Huntingdon?' I replied somewhat angrily. 'And I'm only here now with the compliments of the US Air Force, who flew me up from London. Anyway, sir, that doesn't answer my question. Why are you here?'

'You'd better sit down, Braithwaite,' replied the Group Captain, indicating a chair in front of the desk. 'You see there's been a change of plan since you left Dyce and I am now the CO of this squadron.'

'But, I don't understand, sir,' I said. 'Air Commodore Bennett said this would be my command.'

'Sorry to disappoint you, Braithwaite, I will explain. My name is Group Captain Slee and I've been commanding a station in Lincolnshire for the past six months. They promoted me to group captain after a daylight raid that you probably remember: ninety-seven Lancasters low-level down France to bomb the armament works at Le Creusot, near Vichy, then back by way of the Bay of Biscay.' I did remember; I had done the Pampa in a Spitfire for them. 'Running a bomber station has been rather a bore since then,' Slee continued, 'and when I heard about this special new type of operations, I rang Air Commodore Bennett, who is a friend and contemporary of mine, and asked him for it. It's going to be very important, you know, and he agreed with me that it justified a more experienced and, if you don't mind me saying so, an older man than you. You are only twenty-two, I believe.' Seething, I acknowledged that I was only twenty-two. 'So where do I actually come into this, sir?' I asked. 'I was a squadron commander until Air Commodore Bennett acquired my Mosquitoes out of Coastal; I came with them on the promise of being a squadron commander again; that was ruled out some-where high up, and I had to return as the bad boy to an angry Coastal Command. Perpetual oblivion awaited me there, and Air Commodore Bennett has rescued me with the offer of this squadron. You have the advantage of knowing what it is going to do but once again I get told I'm to be a flight commander, which was why I was sent back to Coastal in the first place. I know about my age, but I also know I have run one of the most successful squadrons in the whole of Coastal Command, I have flown Mosquitoes for well over a year and, from what you have said, you have no experience yet on Mosquitoes, sir. The two types of operation are totally different.'

'That may be,' said Slee, 'but I have much more flying experience than you. I will assimilate very quickly and will rely on you to provide the expertise, which Bennett assures me you have, to advise me on the correct operational procedures.' He went on. 'The other flight commander is also new to these planes, so your importance to this unit will be immense.' Then, putting a sting in the tail, he added: 'If it wasn't for that, of course I would have been nominating my own choice for flight commander. Naturally, if you prefer not to take up the appointment, I am sure I can have a word with Air Commodore Bennett and he will no doubt think of something else for you. If you stay, however, I am sure that you will get the promotion to wing commander that you expected, as I am a Group Captain and almost all the Pathfinder squadrons have wing commander flight commanders.'

I was not sure I believed that, as clearly, if he had not turned up nobody was going to make me a group captain. Nevertheless, realising that my alternative would probably be a post as a flight commander on heavy bombers, for which I had little stomach, with a statistical average of fifteen trips before the coffin or the POW camp, I decided to accept the situation with as much grace as possible.

Slee directed me to 'B' Flight to meet the outgoing flight commander. 139 Squadron had until then operated out of 2 Group, making daring low-level daylight sorties against specific enemy targets, the Philips works at Eindhoven, the marshalling yards at Maastricht, the Gestapo HQ in Copenhagen to mention just a few. Their operations were spectacular and they hit the newspaper headlines every raid, feeding the public with a little success and optimism at a time when they had little else to cheer about.

The Americans had entered the air war with their Flying Fortresses and Liberators equipped for precision daylight bombing, and armed to the teeth with guns for aerial battle against the German daylight fighter fleets. The role of 139 Squadron had become redundant. At this time Bennett was asking for an extension of his command in order to add a further feature to his already successful Pathfinder force, and 139 Squadron was therefore allocated to him.

Apart from two so called 'Oboe' Mosquito squadrons, which had sophisticated radar that directed individual aircraft by cross-beams from England, sufficient to carry Pathfinder target marking to the nearer continental targets such as the Ruhr, the remainder of the force was composed of the four-engined heavy bomber squadrons, Stirlings and Lancasters, Halifaxes and Manchesters. The crews were picked as the very best from all the other heavy bomber squadrons in Bomber Command. It was their job to use their experience, added to their unlimited-range radar, called H2S which I believe is something rude in chemical terminology, designated so by a senior unbeliever in the new gadget. This reflected flat surfaces such as rivers, roads and housetops, thus giving a pictorial view of the ground below, through any cloud, upon which to drop route marking flares, and finally target indicator flares, at the head of and backing up within the main bomber stream. The other bombers, regardless of their own navigational calculations, had to work from these flares. Backing up was necessary, because to put 500 – 700 bombers over a target meant a tightly packed stream of aircraft taking over half an hour to pass through the target, and the flares had to be continually 'topped up' before each burnt out.

By autumn 1943, Bennett had transformed the effectiveness of Bomber Command from a 10 per cent accuracy rate to about 70 per cent, but losses of experienced crews were mounting, owing to the increasing efficiency of the German night-fighter fleets. Aerial countermeasures were called for, and 139 Squadron was designated to introduce them.

What Bennett had decided on is best described with a military analogy, that of the cavalry. He already had the 'Heavy Brigade', the main stream guided by the Pathfinder squadrons. What he needed now was a 'Light Brigade' for the kind of flanking and diversionary tactics that have been used over the centuries since long before aerial warfare was even thought about.

Wyton was another permanent prewar RAF station, with the usual configuration of hangars and buildings, but it also had excellent full-length tarmac runways, a far cry from the hazardous grass field at Bircham Newton. It had 83 Squadron with Lancasters on it, with a Group Captain commanding. The Station Commander was one of three well-known RAF brothers called Jarman. This one was exceedingly short and, like many short men, very self-conscious about it. He used to walk around the station with a swagger stick under his arm. When he was not using it to illustrate a point, he said it was to differentiate him from the other group captain on his station, whom he clearly did not like having there at all. Now he was getting yet another one.

By the time Slee and I arrived, the crews were already talking about 'Bennett's private air force'. As it involved night flying,

The aircrew of No. 521 Squadron. Shown left to Right: Back Row: Flight Sergeant Brown, Sergeant Ashworth, Sergeant Buddle, Sergeant Fry, Sergeant Workman, Sergeant Clayton, Sergeant Swinbanks and Sergeant Bernstein. Centre Row: Pilot Officer Woodruff, Pilot Officer Kelly, Sergeant Burgess, Sergeant Bell, Sergeant Parkinson, Sergeant Boyle, Sergeant Wilson, Sergeant Fettes, Sergeant Swift, Sergeant Raine, Flight Sergeant Durrant, Warrant Officer Griffiths and Pilot Officer Taylor. Front Row Seated: Pilot Officer Watts, Flying Officer Pethick, Flying Officer Green, Flight Lieutenant C-Lister, Squadron Leader Braithwaite, Flying Officer Bispham, Flying Officer Hall, Pilot Officer Butchart and Pilot Officer Crosby.

Flying Officer Green and the Author at 'Immediate Standby' for a PAMPA call.

The flying kit included a Mae West, flying helmet, goggles, oxygen mask and radio-telephone attachments.

Flying Officer Green demonstrates the 'bombing posture' in the nose of a Mosquito.

Flying Officer 'Basher' Bispham, Flying Officer 'Gurt' Green, DFC, the Author and Flight Lieutenant 'Blister' Cunliffe-Lister when No. 521 Squadron was based at Bircham Newton.

Flight Lieutenant Hon. Philip I Cunliffe-Lister who joined No. 521 Squadron in July 1942. On 28 August 1942, he glided an unarmed Spitfire Mk V home with a seized engine from a position near Tours in France. He flew the aircraft at best gliding speed, 132 mph, in a cloudless sky and avoiding enemy fighter patrols for over 200 miles to land safely at Gatwick. He moved with 1409 Flight to the Pathfinders in April 1943 and succeeded the Author as Officer Commanding on 5 May. He was awarded the DSO in June and became a prisoner of war on 18 July.

Flying Officer C H L 'Lance' Dennis climbing into the cockpit of a Spitfire Mk V prior to a 'local'. He broke his back whilst attempting to land a high-altitude Spitfire with a seized engine in bad weather conditions. He broke cloud too far from the aerodrome and spun into the ground where the aircraft exploded. He was fortunate to escape death and eventually rejoined 1409 Flight in the Pathfinders once his back had healed.

Flying Officer 'Old Man' Tilley, so named by an aircraftman who had once asked 'Who was the "very old" pilot getting out of the aircraft?'

Ground crewmen Sergeant Hebron and Corporal Hutchinson stand by a Mosquito that is running-up for a pre-dawn take-off on a PAMPA mission for the United States Army Air Force.

Philip Cunliffe-Lister and the Author.

A de Havilland Mosquito IV with a Perspex 'blister' on the escape hatch. It was experimented with to see if it would improve the rearward vision and thus aid the detection of attacking enemy fighters.

1409 Flight aircrew at RAF Oakington. Left to right. Back Row: Sergeant Bernstein, Sergeant Boyle, Flight Sergeant Clayton, Sergeant Durrant and Sergeant Burgess. Front Row: Pilot Officer Woodruff, Pilot Officer Taylor, Flying Officer Hatton, Flight Lieutenant C-Lister, the Author, Flying Officer Green, Flying Officer Pethick and Flying Officer Dennis.

few of the intrepid and fearless daylight pilots of 139 Squadron wanted anything to do with it. The outgoing flight commander of 'B' Flight told me he was leaving me his splendid 'V' for Victory and that a man called Maule Colledge was staying as a tried and trusted No. 2. His navigator was also departing, so my request for Bob Taylor seemed very timely and he arrived at Wyton the day after I did. However, he explained that he had not been in a plane since being shot down in France, and he was very apprehensive about his possible reaction to flying at height again. I arranged for him to go on a re-familiarisation course, partly to learn how to use the new navigational equipment, the gee box, but more important, to be treated gently and weaned back to high-altitude flying.

In the meantime I started to get some night-flying practice in myself, as I was about as disturbed by it as the outgoing 139 crews were. Frankly, until I got there I had completely forgotten that I did not know how to fly at night! It turned out to be more difficult in theory than it was in practice, however. But, V Victory was dreadful. Its controls were so sharp that it had to be flown every inch of the way, maybe a good idea for low-level daylight bombing through overhead power lines, ever-narrowing streets with tram cables above etc., but most uncomfortable for a lengthy trip through the night hours, when accuracy of speed and direction were all important for good navigation.

Imagine, then, my astonishment and delight when I went down to my flight office one morning to find dear old S for Sugar, DZ 359, parked right outside my window, having been extensively reconditioned by de Havillands and then sent to 139 Squadron as a replacement. I claimed her immediately and thenceforward she became R for Robert, the nearest I could get to S for Sugar. I also had a plaque painted on the side of the cockpit and had her twenty-one Pampa Flights inserted in the squares, to be followed thereafter by bombs for ordinary targets and special bombs for Berlin.

While I was waiting for Bob to return I started to gain operational experience with anyone who might be available. Flying Officer Ulrich Cross was one of my first navigators. He was jet black, a Trinidadian and I believe ultimately the most decorated West Indian of the war. The problem was that one felt quite alone flying with Ulrich, because one looked in his direction, one saw nothing owing to the blackness behind the helmet, oxygen mask and goggles. 'Please look at me Ulrich' had become a common pilot's saying. Only the whites of his eyes were able to reassure you that you were not on your own. The first time we went up together, on a short Cologne 'milk run', Ulrich said 'Please hurry up, sir, as best you can. I have a date in Cambridge at 8.30.' No wonder they win the test matches!

A week later, Bob Taylor returned from his re-familiarisation course. As soon as I saw him I said, 'Great – there's an easy op on tonight on the Ruhr. Just the thing to get you back into the swing of things. Go to ops and get the gen and we'll meet at flights in an hour.' In the plane, everything seemed fine, but it was not. As we climbed up to about 25,000 feet over the Dutch coast, before any flak or other sign of opposition, Bob suddenly threw his navigational chartboard, maps, pencils etc., away from him and his arms started flailing; he was clearly right out of control. I turned the plane around and into a dive back to lower altitudes and base. Once back, he gradually recovered and told me tearfully that his re-familiarisation had involved sitting on his backside, with one flight up to 5,000 feet. I had not given him a chance to tell me and he had not wanted to let me down. God bless Phil Hazleman, he got Bob the perfect job, as senior navigational officer at our navigation school in Nova Scotia, Canada, for the rest of the war.

A few days later I had my first operation on Berlin, taking Squadron Leader Evans, the Squadron Navigation Officer with me. The battle order consisted of eight aircraft. As it was nearly a full moon, the heavies could not operate; bright moonlight made them too vulnerable to night fighters. Therefore our job was purely to prevent the defences and the civilian population from getting a good night's rest. The route out, across Holland, was made difficult by heavy thunderstorms to a depth of 40 or 50 miles inland. Four aircraft turned back and Colledge and Marshal were never heard from again. I was hit four times near Hanover, but without significant damage, and was then coned from Brandenburg onward, taking a real pasting, with ten direct hits. That was the night that two pieces of shrapnel, which I keep as a memento, fell out of my flying suit when I took it off after the flight.

Berlin had a sufficient density of searchlights and anti-aircraft guns so that no matter what a heavy did they could guarantee a direct hit by firing a great simultaneous pattern at one plane. This applied much less to the Mosquitoes, as they flew 10,000 feet higher. What the defence actually did was to get the targets into an apex of twenty or thirty searchlights, then all the gunners simply let fly, up the funnel. It was highly unnerving to be at the top of it, whether a heavy or a light bomber. It used to take a shell one second per 1,000 feet to reach its target, so the heavies had twenty seconds to alter course and height sufficiently to avoid being hit, assuming the German gunners had worked out the direction, height and speed of the aircraft properly. With Mosquitoes we had the extra ten seconds. One problem, however, was that aircraft were expected to maintain course, speed and height until their bombs reached the ground – approximately the same time lapse – so that a photoflash which went with the bombs would be picked up by the plane's vertical camera and so show what we managed to hit or not hit.

Two nights later, Pilot Officer Joe Patient and Sergeant Gilroy were on their fourth operation, the target again Berlin. We waited up for them in the Interrogation Room until 3.30am., when their fuel must have long gone, and then we all went off to bed.

The following morning, I wandered down to the flight office wondering how to reorganise things now that Joe had had it – who would take over as Sports Officer, who was going to stick the pins in the flight record map that Joe had got into such a state of confusion that I could not imagine anybody else understanding it. I opened the office door, and if the saying 'shaken rigid' has an interpretation it fitted them.

Joe said, 'I bet you didn't expect to find me here.'

'Hell,' I answered, 'what are you doing here? I thought you were tramping through the Black Forest or somewhere like that by now.'

'No,' said Joe, 'but I'm sorry, sir, S for Sugar has had it.' Then he told me the story.

Like the rest of us, S for Sugar had had a fairly stiff passage through the storms over Holland, and again four out of the seven aircraft had turned back. Once clear of the storms however, the rest of us had pressed on uneventfully to the target. As he dropped his bombs, as Joe put it, 'Every bloody bastard in the place decided to fix Joseph J. Patient.' In front, behind, above and below they came. 'They're bursting on our starboard wingtip,' shouted Gilroy; 'Turn port.'

'Turning starboard,' shouted Joe, 'they can't be as bad that side as they are this.' Alas, they were, and Joe's starboard engine soon went for a rapid purler. 'Things are in a mess,' said Joe. 'There we were, a couple of blinking sprogs, six hundred miles from a cup of tea, a damn great moon, night fighters, flak, bad weather between us and home, and one bloody engine, and, what's more, bloody little petrol as the starboard tank is now cut off, as it doesn't transfer to the port engine and I have forgotten to use the outer tanks first.'

Well, Joe decided that what petrol he did have available was not enough to take them home on the northern route that the rest of the squadron were taking back over the North Sea, so they had better go straight home over the route they had come in on. So they turned west and, slowly losing height, left Berlin behind. Gilroy worked out a nice course to take them between all the defended areas, but unfortunately this was not very successful because they had scarcely received their last farewells from Berlin when Bremen began to have a go. Joe did the wrong thing now, throwing S for Sugar all over the sky, 'fighting the searchlights'. This is a pretty fruitless idea at the best of times, even when one is not trying to eek out every foot of height because the aircraft has one engine working. 17,000 feet out of his original 30,000 feet only were left when he finally managed to leave Bremen behind, luckily no worse off. Owing to an error in judging where they had actually flown over, he now flew straight into the Wilhelmshaven defences, where an exact repetition of Bremen took place. After this Gilroy got a good idea of where he was, which was much too far to the north, and immediately ordered a change of course to the south, just in time to fly, at 11,000 feet straight over Emden. Amazingly, they once again came through unscathed, though by now hopelessly lost.

The petrol situation was now beginning to look a little hopeless, but they carried on in a south-westerly direction, their height was now 7,000 feet. The moon was still hanging high in the sky, and there were no signs of friendly cloud cover. From calculations afterwards, it was estimated that they were approximately over Utrecht, in southern Holland, when Joe suddenly saw what looked like streams of shooting stars go whistling over the top of the cockpit, coming from directly behind. He pushed the stick hard forward, and then skidded the aircraft up again to starboard. The shooting stars had stopped, but sitting quietly on his port wingtip was a beautifully moonlit Focke Wulf 190. Joe's words are unprintable, but they met the situation quite adequately and were accompanied by a steep turn into the other aircraft. This must have shaken the German, as badly as it would have shaken Joe had he had time to realise what he was attempting to do; nevertheless, the pilot managed to get out of the way in time, and next moment Joe found him sitting on his starboard wingtip. This made Joe so angry that he immediately did the same thing again; presumably the German thought he must be mad, because he was not to be seen any more.

He was now at just 500 feet and as he settled down for the last stages of the journey to the coast, he suddenly found that petrol was pouring out of the aircraft from his central tanks which, a quarter full, were all he had left; his last chance of getting home was gone. He could now recognise the Low Countries beneath, and he held a quick consultation with Gilroy as to whether to reach the coast, fly down it to the Straits of Dover and then, if they were still going, try to get across, or whether to hope for a miracle and try to make the English coast direct. They decided on the latter course, and crossed out into the North Sea after another short duel with the coastal light flak, this time at 100 feet, with 15 gallons left showing on the petrol gauge, enough to take them nicely out in the middle of a very cold North Sea, 40 miles if they were lucky, before the engine stopped. Joe therefore proposed to climb steadily from the coast until he reached a height of 5,000 feet. At this height he would continue flying toward England until the gauges read empty. Then Gilroy would bale out, Joe would circle him until he ran out of petrol, and would then ditch beside him in the sea.

He reached 5,000 feet and set an accurate course point on the English coastline. It so happened that in the battering they had received, the only electrical instrument left working in the aircraft was also the most delicate, the Gee box. Once they were over the North Sea and back at 5,000 feet Gee would give them their exact position at any moment. When Joe told Gilroy to get out, Gilroy said, 'no damned fear, we're so close to England now that I'm damned if I propose to jump into the middle of the North Sea.' So with no petrol left showing on the gauges they watched the English searchlights begin to flicker on the horizon. Gilroy sent out every emergency call there was on the wireless, but there was no reply as the wireless was dead. The solitary engine drummed on, and never can two people have waited more anxiously, listening with every nerve in the bodies, for the dreaded splutter that would herald the failure of their remaining engine.

The coastline searchlights grew brighter second by second and they were now so close that they could see the red flashing beacon of an aerodrome in front of then. Then, like a miracle, out of the darkness the great illuminated cartwheel of a night-landing system was suddenly switched on. Joe shouted, 'Gilroy, they've heard us, that's for us. I'm going right in.' As he turned in on the aerodrome, anywhere or anyhow on it, with no navigation or identification lights to warn anyone, his engine cut dead, the last of his fuel gone. After a silent, ghostlike approach, S for Sugar skidded to a halt on its belly right across the aerodrome flarepath, in the full glare of the dazzling take-off chance light some hundreds of yards away to the left, at the head of the runway. Illuminated by the chance light they looked at each other and wondered if it really was true, that they really were back home. Then S for Sugar exploded.

That moment will also be remembered by the pilot of Q Queenie, a Tempest night-fighter. He was tail up, rushing down the familiar flare path, about to feel the ground slide away beneath him at any moment, and then, point-blank in front of him he saw a large aircraft glide gracefully to a full stop. The next moment he ploughed straight through it and finished up on his nose on the far side.

Joe sat in a chair to the side of my desk, puffing away hard at his cigarette, silent for a moment as he finished his story, then said, 'Oh, sir, I've brought you a copy of the preliminary report on S for Sugar.'

Fuselage: From roundels to tail gone.
Port Engine: 5 ft gash in nacelle and engine housing caused by cannon shells from astern.

Starboard Engine: Destroyed by flak.

Petrol Tanks: All tanks, except starboard outer well perforated by cannon shells and empty. Starboard outer full.

Hydraulic system and main wireless and lighting system: U/s, damaged by German action.

Cockpit: Perforated by six machine-gun bullets entering within 1 in of observer's head, and passing out on opposite side, ½ in behind position of pilot's neck.

The last item of damage was afterwards determined to have been done simultaneously with FW 190 attack by a second aircraft, as Joe said he remembered a slight breeze around the nape of his neck about that time.

There was a polite knock on the door, and Gilroy came in. He turned to Patient. 'Have you asked him yet?'

'No,' replied Joe.

'Excuse me, sir, but on the drive back here this morning Gilroy and I were talking it over, and we felt a bit narked about all this and were wondering if you could fix it so that we could take somebody's place on the battle order tonight. It's the Big Smoke again and we'd rather like to get our own back.'

'Sorry,' I replied, 'but I think the best thing for you is a good spot of weekend leave, and that's what you're getting.'

In the second half of September the moon had begun to wane, allowing the heavies to commence operating again. Now the second side of our work began which was to go with the heavies, though higher and faster, arriving simultaneously with their vanguard at a prearranged position. We then generally altered course, with us going off in the direction of another diversionary target and them continuing to the real one.

For a long time, enemy radar defences had been blinded by the heavies dropping bundles of tinsel, similar to the silver strips used for Christmas tree decorations. These were pushed out through a chute in the bottom of each plane, thousands of tinsel strips floated down, each bundle of 2,000 giving off a radar reflection similar to that of an aeroplane, and effective for six or seven minutes. Now we were also using these tinsel bundles, which were named 'window', the joke order to our navigator's being to 'Window till exhausted' and indeed it was exhausting work having to open dozens of brown paper packages full of Window bundles and keep stuffing them down the chute in the floor without stopping for a half an hour or more. In this way, our few aircraft could pretend to be the main force and delay the German fighter controllers for vital minutes before they could make up their minds and commit their fleets to the correct target, so enabling many bombers to get through.

Of course we would drop our 500 lb bombs on our diversionary target, thus increasing our nuisance value when we are operating without the heavies.

The German night-fighter forces were of two kinds, the larger being the fleet operations, and the smaller, the ground control interception defence boxes, where pairs of planes were under controlled direction, each in a specific area 70 miles long by 20 miles wide, to pick up individual aircraft, often stragglers, in the coastal areas facing England.

The fleets would be ordered into the air as the route of a raid progressed. The time they could stay airborne was very limited, so they were carefully directed from marker beacon to marker beacon, converging on the ultimate target, and meanwhile conserving their fuel as much as possible. If we could draw them off to follow the diversionary force, all to the good. Then they might not be able to get back to the right target at all, or at least their available time for attack would be reduced.

We had radio transmitters working on the German Command frequencies. Our operators knew where we were and where we were going. They would tell the German pilots that the bombers had changed course and that the target was now confirmed as, say, Hamburg and to go there at top speed. The German controller would say, 'Don't pay any attention to that; that is the Englishman.' The English controller would come back, 'That was the English controller. I am your controller and I order you to proceed to Hamburg.' This would cause great confusion. One night there were 400 fighters circling the Bremen beacon at 18,000 feet on a clockwise circuit. The British controller had a brilliant idea. 'All aircraft orbiting Beacon B to orbit anti-clockwise.' Many collisions were reported. Another trick was to say: 'All squadrons from these airfields return to base immediately. Weather deteriorating fast. Fog conditions expected within thirty minutes.' This always took a few faint-hearted pilots back home, but it was far worse if that actually was the German order, as most pilots would be convinced that it was the British controller and ignore it.

Getting the German fighter fleet to the correct target became very difficult but eventually they thought they had found the way to get it right. In the middle of the exchanges, and without any warning, a female announcer suddenly came on the air. But we had thought of that, too, and our female voice responded immediately. That simply finished as a cat fight over the air, no doubt to the great annoyance of all the German pilots who never had that sense of humour anyway.

They did eventually solve the problem by teaching all their aircrew famous pieces of music. When they had positively identified the main target they would play music, say the 'Vienna Waltz' for Berlin or the 'Blue Danube' for Mannheim, and the German pilots would consult their chart for the night and fly off to the right target. As we were concentrating on some fifty cities in Germany we hoped that there were pilots that became confused and went the wrong way or so we hoped.

Ground-controlled interception (GCI) boxes were about two deep around the coastline from the north of Holland to the Belgian-French border. Each had the two standard German radars, the Freya and the Würtzburg, and two aircraft, all controlled by a major. It took an undamaged bomber seven or eight minutes to fly through a box, and therefore a German fighter at full throttle had a chance to catch it within his territorial limit if he was well positioned at the start. However, if he did not have visual contact before it passed out through his boundary, the fighter had to break off, such was the German inflexability, and, passing an interception to the next box controller was a very formal procedure. Nevertheless, a fighter achieving a closing speed of 100 mph could make up 13 miles in the allotted time, and much more if the bomber were returning home against a strong wind. These boxes caused serious problems to all our bombers, and particularly to damaged stragglers on their way home.

After a few weeks the situation began to become clearer so far as our operations were concerned. In moonlight on our own, if we could be seen from the ground, we were sitting ducks and could reasonably be expected to take serious losses. In the dark periods we were there to draw off the German fighter fleet, and our diversionary targets were often places that did not have the major defences of the largest German cities. Nevertheless, whether damaged or not, we had to pass through the GCI boxes on the way out and mostly on the way home too. Moreover, bad weather seemed to turn back far too many of our crews. Compared with daylight reconnaissance work, we were not doing well, but there, relying so much on speed, we flew at an average of 300 mph against the 250 mph stipulated for Pathfinder Mosquitoes.

Group Captain Slee had by this time settled down to a routine of running the administrative side of the squadron and then mostly returning to Cambridge, where I could contact him if there was a good raid to go on, or anything else I thought needed his personal attention. I therefore brought up the matter of our operating speed with him, and when I had proved to him by doing a Berlin trip at the higher speed without using more fuel than the other aircraft, he became quite obsessed with the idea. I later discovered that he took the decision on himself and the squadron's operations were immediately changed to the higher speeds. This resulted in a dramatic change in our success rate. The planes were more manoeuvrable now and got through the bad weather where they could not before. Losses were reduced almost to nil, and confidence grew and grew.

There were of course individual occurences. On one raid Slee came on the radio (which we were not really meant to use over target), 'Denys, 'he said, 'do you see that poor bugger over there getting shot to hell?'

Looking across the Berlin night sky, I saw a plane with sixty search lights on it and every German gunner within range trying out his skill.

'Yes,' I replied, 'I can see him, Leonard. I wonder who the poor sod is.'

'Me,' came the reply,

I had a rough experience on a raid over Hamburg. George Hodder, now my permanent navigator, used to say little once we had passed into hostile territory except to remind me occasionally of his wife and two children. But when the port engine failed he agreed with me that we were so close to target that we should go on and drop our little load along with the heavy bomber stream. We were down to about 18,000 feet going in, and a heavy got a direct hit and blew up, bomb load and all, right in front of us. It was so close that I could not avoid flying straight through the huge orange ball; we could smell the burning flesh. We had seen many German 'scarecrow' pyrotechnics, magnificent imitations of bombers falling out of the sky, blowing up bit by bit as they went down, which were frightening to our crews, but great morale boosters to the German anti-aircraft crews. But, this was no scarecrow; it was quite horrible.

Once clear of the target area, we proceeded north with the main bomber stream up to Sylt in Denmark, then turned west for England. Now our troubles started. There was a very strong westerly wind of about 80 knots against us and a nasty weather front that we had passed over without trouble on the outward journey. Now we had to go back at a much lower altitude, through the front at a painfully slow speed because of wind and the lost engine. The tops of the front, at 19,000 feet, had a lot of icing condition and we were faced with a problem. If we tried to stay above the cloud we were unable to hold course and gradually turned in to the Lofoten Islands along the north coast of Germany, which were well defended. Crunch, crunch, up came the flak, far too close for our peace of mind. So I would put down the nose, increase speed, turn back north, away from the shell bursts, then clunk, clunk, clunk, the ice off the propeller rattled down the sides of the plane. The lower we went, the more icing we got and the slower we flew. We then climbed up again, above the cloud, lost speed, veered south, and the AA guns started up again. This went on for a painful two hours until at last, off the north of Holland, we flew out into clear skies and were able to reduce to a more reasonable height and fly home in peace. 'Mayday, mayday,' I heard over the air, 'I'm on two engines and request emergency landing instructions.' I just couldn't resist responding. 'What the hell are you complaining about, I've been on one engine for the past two and a half hours.' I did not tell him of course that I was only flying a twin-engined plane. He didn't bother to answer.

As old hands, we became very blasé about new crews arriving. 'He's OK, but look at the other fellow, far too nice and gentle, he'll not make half a tour,' we said about a man called

Mellor. He belonged to the other flight and was given three nights in a row on Berlin. He didn't return, which did not surprise us but we were quite astounded when he arrived back some eleven weeks later, having walked from Berlin to Gibraltar and evaded capture all the way. Moreover he had not been shot down; both engines had broken down, one with a coolant leak and the other an oil leak!

The other flight commander, Squadron Leader Skene, had joined 139 at the beginning of the previous June. Much older than me, he was a very disciplined man, without a shade of humour about him, and without any ability to instill enthusiasm in his crews whatsoever. He was clearly a good, solid administrator, but boring to a degree. We got on because we never crossed paths which was probably his skillful doing, because I could not have thought that out. His flying record in the squadron made it quite clear that he was pacing himself. After thirty operational trips he was likely to be termed 'tour expired' and he wanted to stay around a long time, so he did an operation just every so often. The fact that he'd send Mellor out three times in a row did not mean that he himself was not prepared to go; it meant that it was not time for him to operate again that week.

On one occasion Leonard Slee, once again announcing his presence to all and sundry, called out, 'Denys, do you see the heavy 20 miles or so south of us, being coned by searchlights?' We were then halfway home, to the north of the heavily defended Rhur region.

I had already seen the poor chap and it was clear that he was just flying straight and level and taking no evasive action. 'Yes, I'm watching him.' I replied.

'In a minute, he's dead,' predicted Slee. 'He's flying right into the Osnabrück defences.'

Something nudged my memory back to a Hudson, going around again at Wick three long years before, with Hilary Duke-Wooley predicting the disaster that happened there. Just then two or three shells burst around the nose of the plane. Then there was a cascade of bursts, simultaneously and it was all over in a second. The aircraft started to burn from the front, the fire spreading rapidly down the fuselage, and the nose tilted down and down until it was a vertical trail of fire. I often wondered about that plane. There were probably six men in the crew. Were they all already dead and the plane on automatic gyro compass just flying on west till its fuel gave out? Or had they already baled out? Or were they all lying around injured, dead or unconscious, with just one desperate and brave wireless operator trying to bring the plane back to England single handed? Whatever, that was the end of a four-engined bomber, and on average it happened to over six of them out of every hundred every time they operated.

There were surprises. Once George and I almost ran into balloons in the Ruhr. George had already gone into the nose to prepare for bombing and never saw the three enormous balloons. I had to do a very fast climbing turn to avoid them – this at 27,000 feet. I flew around in a circle to try to pick them up again, but could not. George had not seen them, so it was not until the war was over that my sighting was confirmed: three balloons holding up to one cable between them. Nobody else saw them, but I wonder how many planes were actually grabbed out of the sky by that cable. My report received no comment whatsoever; I suppose that they all thought, in Group HQ, that I had started to have hallucinations!

On another occasion, four of our Canadian pilots gave us all a surprise. As we went into the attack on the target for the night, all four started up in unison with 'Lay that pistol down, babe, lay that pistol down.' The rest of us thought it was great fun and wondered if the Germans who were listening appreciated it too.

One night, George and I had the most extraordinary flight. It was going to be a completely clear night, with no moon whatsoever. The heavies were on Berlin in force and we were putting up our usual diversion for them. I requested permission to arrive on the main target forty minutes after the raid was over, in order to cause some extra confusion. It was quite amazing. As we climbed up to height over the North Sea we saw the raid start, almost 500 miles away, as though it were under our nose. The visibility was such that we could have seen a light in Poland, were it not for the curvature of the Earth. We watched everything, the early target indicators going down, the early bombing, the planes being coned, the flak going up, aircraft going down or exploding, the German scarecrows making it even more spectacular, and the fires and explosions on the ground becoming more intense as the raid progressed. Then the firing began to die down, the searchlights gradually flickered out. All that was left when we got there, forty minutes later, were huge fires, many very spectacular, over vast areas in the middle of the city.

Nobody, paid the least attention to us. The defences were all closing down so George and I meandered right across the city as far as the Warsaw Gate. One the way, down below, we saw a great transport plane silhouetted against the fires. It was circling round, and we decided it was Goering having a look for himself. What a pity it was that we didn't have any guns!

Then, we decided where we wanted our bombs to go and George got down into the nose to set the bomb sights. I cannot remember what George's fire looked like but mine was a great curling emerald green affair. Then we flew all the way back home without a single pot shot being taken at us from anywhere. It might as well have been a scenic flight in a peace-time airliner.

Our intelligence received information very quickly and by the time we reached the Interrogation Room back home they knew that we had hit the University in the Unter den Linden with the first pair of bombs, and an underground station, also in the Unter den Linden, with the second. We hit the latter as civilians were pouring out of it, as it was used during raids as an air-raid shelter, and there were rather a lot of casualties. This was total war however, so what today might seem awful was not regarded as such at that time. Later on, the ploy of putting pairs of Mosquitoes on target at varying times after a raid was over became a fairly standard practice, although I hope they did not hit too many evacuating underground stations.

One night I was doing duty as Interrogation Officer for the Mosquitoes. They had made a diversionary attack somewhere, and had all got back before the first of the heavy crews came in. The latter were shattered to say the least. The Germans had waited to see which route they would take leaving the target and then in had come squadrons of JU 88s and laid four lanes of 6,000,000 candle-power parachute flares, 15 miles, wide and 60 miles long. This lit up the bombers almost to daylight levels, and the night fighters went in and shot down many bombers.

Air Commodore Bennett was in the Interrogation Room and immediately sent for Slee and Skene to join us. 'How many aircraft can you put up 9.00a.m. tomorrow?' He asked. We agreed we could manage sixteen. 'Right,' said Bennett, and took out a map of the British Isles. 'We'll divide the country in sixteen. You will land at every station of any sort that could possibly have flares. When you have found the flares, we will send a Lancaster for them. We want them tomorrow. Do you all understand?' We did, and the next morning sixteen Mosquitoes took off to scour the country. At 4.00 p.m. forty-eight 1,500,000 candle-power parachute flares were located at Pershore in Worcestershire. A Lancaster had them back at Wyton at high speed. Whether it worked out scientifically or not, I do not know, but four were tied together to make one, and four of these were loaded into each of three aircraft.

The night's target was again Berlin and the bomber route away from the target was north towards Denmark, as it generally was. Our three aircraft were piloted by myself, my room mate Murray Mitchell from Toronto, and Smokey Stovel, another great Canadian from Winnipeg. At absolutely precise timing we flew directly east out of the target area. I dropped four flares in a line. Mitchell did the same a few hundred yards to my right and parallel. Mine immediately were followed up by four more from Smokey – not bad with no scientific navigational aids from Holland onwards. The next moment, along came the JU 88s and soon the night sky was illuminated halfway to Poland; in came the night fighters, but they naturally found no bombers; we had got away with it completely.

The next night we had a full supply of 6,000,000 candle-power parachute flares and thereafter it became another radio argument between command controllers: 'the northerly flare path is the English one,' 'No, it isn't,' and so on. The JU 88s had to wait until the controllers had made up their minds, and then the fighters had to wait till the JU 88s had laid their flare paths.

Looking back there was scarcely an operational night when something did not happen to increase the adrenalin flow. There was the night when twelve of us were taking off just after dark and climbing up over Norwich, arriving there at 11,000 feet, when a like number of twin-engined Messerschmitts, which looked very like Mosquitoes in the dark, came diving down to bomb the city at the same height. At the same time, two squadrons of night-fighter Mosquitoes arrived to intercept them from the north. Thus, there were fifty or sixty of us all in the same place at the same moment, all going in different directions. Tracer bullets and aeroplanes flashed past from everywhere. We fired off our night-time recognition Very pistols for all the good they would do; we were probably firing German signals, even though we were always instructed last thing before take-off. 'Remember not to change to the enemy signals till you cross the coast.' I am sure our navigators always put the German signal cartridges in straight away. Likewise, the opposition was busy firing off our signals and the only people with the right one would have been the night-fighter squadrons who were busy firing guns, not Very pistols. I believe that nobody was hurt at all, but it was quite a hair-raising four or five minutes for all that.

Another night, George and I were diverted to Bradwell Bay on our return because the weather had closed in at base. It was a lovely moonlit night at Bradwell Bay, a night intruder base. Before we got out of the plane we were surprised to see quite a few aircrew who were in the tarmac area come over to inspect us, clearly with great admiration. It was only after we got out that we realised what it was all about. In the moonlight R for Robert's twenty-odd Met. flights, denoted by a jagged stroke of lightning on the panel on the port side of the cockpit looked for all the world like swastikas denoting enemy aircraft shot down. We were loath to disillusion our fan club, but as we wanted them to feed us and give us a bed for the night we reluctantly did so; having spun it out as long as we could by pretending we did not know what it was all about. One chap was even looking around for some paper to get our autographs!

When I was returning from one trip I found my hydraulics had gone, so I did not have any flaps or brakes with which to stop when I landed. I therefore diverted to Wittering, an aerodrome to the west side of the old Great North Road north of Stamford. I always remembered it because as a small boy, when the family passed it in the car, there was always a big plane that had crashed into the ditch between the road and the edge of the aerodrome. I used to think it was an advertisement for the RAF but felt it was probably counter-productive. It was there for a long time but it had long gone the night I approached the great emergency runway as slowly as I could. I touched down directly over the boundary fence and then started to trundle along the immense length of flare path ahead of me. There was no wind and we just kept going and going, and the end of the flare path got closer and closer. At 100 yards I put my hand on the under-carriage retraction lever. I had no intention of finishing in the ditch or quarry that runways generally have at the end of them. At 50 yards I released the safety button. At 20 yards, my hand started to move – and then the control tower switched on the next 5,000 yards of flare path, just in the nick of time.

One afternoon I was sitting in my flight office with my back to the window that faced the airfield. Next door was the Navigation Office and Evans, the Navigator Officer, was sitting there likewise. An orange light lit up the office, followed by an enormous explosion. I was under my desk before the glass of the window blew in. Evans had got between two large steel filing cabinets, which took four men to move normally and had been positioned against each other until that moment! On the far side of the field the heavies were getting ready to take off, two hours before us. Crews were in their planes and the armourers were setting their fuses on the bombs and making the last checks on things like the magnesium flares. What had happened was that the poor armourer working on a particular Lancaster managed to dislodge a magnesium flare, so that it fell to the ground and exploded. So did the 16,000 lb cookie the plane was carrying. When we looked out to see what had happened there was only a puff of smoke and it was a long time before we realised that there had been one Lancaster that literally was not there any longer. The unfortunate armourer had gone with it, and windows were blown out of three houses 7 miles away. Next door to the parking bay was a Nissen hut, which of course had been flattened. But out of the wreckage crawled the six-man crew, who had been breaking the strictest of operational orders and were playing cards in the hut whilst awaiting take-off, instead of being at their station in the aircraft. How lucky can you get? Well, almost: they were all court martialled for disobeying orders!

On one operation I was detailed to do the night's diversion and then to go to the main target, Mannheim, and photograph the whole of the heavy raid with a brand new type of colour film created for the purpose by Kodak in America at a cost of many thousands of dollars. Everything went according to plan, and my half-hour circuit of Mannheim at varying heights, taking spectacular pictures was superb. I wondered if my name would be on the newsreels all over the world as the intrepid pilot who had done it. When we got back however, we found that the armourer had forgotten to take the cap off the lense cover of the camera!

One morning our Air Officer Commanding, Donald Bennett, now an Air Vice Marshal, treated us to an unusual flying display. He had some brand new engines put into a Beaufighter. How he managed to stay on the runway and get airborne was a miracle as the engines created so much torque, making the plane swerve violently to the left, that it seemed impossible for it to avoid crashing. Though I did not know it, of course, they were the Griffon engines that Rolls-Royce had developed, not much bigger than the Merlins we were using, but about twice as powerful. Bennett was not only the complete expert in every-thing connected with aviation, he was also a superb pilot. Air vice marshal or not, he himself flew every operation he asked his squadron crews to do, as he was not prepared to order people into situations that he had not experienced himself. He flew a Pampa flight and amazed the navigator, known as the secretary by that time, with his vast technical knowledge of practical weather interpretation.

As Christmas approached we seemed to have mastered our 'light cavalry' tasks; we had beaten the Germans, whose guns were not capable of shooting us down, and their night fighters, who could not catch us. The only way we were likely to sustain losses was through something unexpected and even that was not happening very much any more.

Then Group HQ informed us that the squadron would move to a new station nearby at the end of January and that Slee, Skene and I would have finished our tours by then, so it would be an opportune time to replace us with a fresh team. There had been quite a commotion over my previous operational flying; Coastal Command calculated everything in numbers of hours, whilst Bomber Command did their mathematics by numbers of operational sorties. Group Captain Mahaddie in Group HQ finally decided that I qualified as a third-tour man, and therefore that I would be tour expired at twenty-five operations – thirty as a maximum if that fitted the time better.

Then disaster struck. 'The AOC wants to see you straight away', the Adjutant said to me over the phone.

'What about?' I asked.

'Don't know,' he replied, 'something pretty uptight though. You'd better get down there pronto.'

Half an hour later I was standing in front of the Air Vice Marshal.

Without, inviting me to sit down, Bennett said, 'I have just found out that you are operating your squadron contrary to all group instructions. You are flying at 2,650 revs instead of the group regulation 2,250. Also, you have taken all the iceguards off the engine intakes. You will return to your squadron immediately, have all the iceguards replaced before tonight's operations and instruct all crews that they will fly at 2,250 rpm from now on. You will bring forward tonight's take-off times accordingly.'

I was flabbergasted! I knew that this man, quite my hero, must be fully conversant with our operational procedure. He was one of the most meticulous people I had ever met and would have spotted that we were operating at faster speeds the very first night. I was not aware until then that Slee had not cleared it with him when I had requested permission from him, as my squadron commander, well over two months earlier.

'Sir.' I said, 'on the technical side, what we are doing is no different from what we have been doing on Pampa flights for a year or more. The difference amounts to an extra fifty miles per hour, which is vital to prevent interception, and last night we completed our 139th operation without any failure or any loss.'

Bennett broke in, 'Braithwaite, I will not lose an entire squadron one night when it runs out of petrol because you are deliberately flouting group orders.'

'Sir, that will not happen. For all the time I have been flying Mosquitoes, I have had my tanks dipped after every trip so as to be absolutely precise about the amount of fuel I have used, and there is almost no difference in miles per gallon flying at the one speed or the other, because the tail drags at 2,250 whereas the plane flies on a perfectly even keel at 2,650.'

'Braithwaite, I have heard enough. I have given you an order. Go and carry it out.'

I believed that meant telling the crews to start being killed again. It also meant a climb-down in front of everybody, humiliation. Had I been a regular, and this my career, I might have reacted differently – I do not know. But I was not; I held an Auxiliary Air Force commission, and was in for the duration only.

'Sir, I cannot.'

'You are addressing your Air Officer Commanding. I won't have this, Braithwaite.'

'Sir, I will find Group Captain Slee to come to see you. Please give him the order if you have to. You put him in charge of the squadron. In fact, when he is away, Skene is nominated second in command, not me.'

Bennett was livid. Just before I saluted prior to leaving, I added: 'By the way, sir, the iceguards. Your opposite number in Photographic Reconnaissance, whom I know to be a friend of yours, has only this week ordered the scrapping of all iceguards on Mosquitoes in PRU.' The only reply I got was an infuriated tightening of the lips. I saluted and left his office.

Back at the squadron I quickly located Slee at Cambridge. 'Get here as soon as you can, sir. We, or at least I, am in serious trouble.' An hour later, Slee got back and I outlined the problem. 'If Bennett wants to run the squadron himself, let him do it,' I said. 'I'm ready to go.'

'Quite agree with you, Denys. I feel exactly the same. I'll go and see him now.'

What happened at that meeting I never really knew. Suffice to say, we carried on flying at 2,650 rpm and did not put the iceguards back on. Eliminating the iceguards contributed 15 or 20 mph to our increased speed and the extra revs the remainder.

Two weeks later I was seconded to a Bomber Command tactical course, but first I was sent up to 100 Group, the new counter-measures Group, to see if there would be a suitable opening there. They wanted me to start a new tour right away, however, and although Phil Hazleman at the Air Ministry had approached Group HQ offering to take me off their hands, they told him to keep out of it. The upshot was that I received an immediate posting to Training Command HQ, the most miserable posting possible. Acting Squadron Leader Braithwaite to revert to the rank of Flight Lieutenant forthwith.

Why Bennett did what he did I will never know. The orders

he gave me were never carried out. Not long after I left our Mark IV Mosquitoes began to be replaced by more powerful ones fitted with the Griffon engines that he had been testing in that Beaufighter, and thus flew even faster and higher. The history of 139 Squadron's success between then and the end of the war is quite amazing. We really had beaten the enemy. There were no more losses, the squadron developed into a wing, eventually carrying 4,000 lb bombs instead of the 2,000 lb ones we used to carry. Instead of the four or eight aircraft we used to put up, thirty or forty operated together, delivering a poundage of high explosive equivalent to a heavy raid of earlier times, with virtually no loss of aircraft or life whatsoever. Both Slee and Skene left when the squadron departed for Upwood, and I think we could be well satisfied with what we had achieved between us.

As for the air vice marshal, he was a genius in anything connected with flying but geniuses can have whims. I sort of remember Churchill signing a piece of paper that sent two of our finest capital ships to their deaths for no reason that ever got explained. Whatever precipitated this order to me, he was a man who would not be crossed, and when he wrote a book about it all a dozen years later, Slee and I were both pointedly omitted from the credit lines. It was understandable that he should be furious at being challenged by a 22 year old, but the fact that it obviously still rankled so badly so many years later was sad.

The evening that the posting to Training Command came through, I was called to the mess telephone. It was Phil Hazleman. 'I hope this posting on my desk is what you really want,' he said.

'Of course not,' I replied, 'but I suppose I had to expect it. I'm not in Donald Bennett's good books any more.'

'Well, whatever, come and see me in London as soon as you arrive, and we'll see what we can arrange. I have ideas.'

A day later I was in London and went to see him. When I had finished recounting what had happened, he said, 'How about going over to the States and flying the first Canadian-built Mosquito across the Atlantic, breaking the speed record and so on?'

'Phil, that would be a splendid idea. I'm sure we have enough fuel capacity for it, but I can check that from my own figures in a few hours.'

CHAPTER SEVEN

America

And so it was that I caught the SS *Aquitania* from the Clyde on 8 February 1944. I arrived in New York on the 17th and two days later took the overnight train north. The following morning, as the train was pulling into Montreal station I was standing in the corridor when the man next to me said, 'Where are your earmuffs?' When I told him I did not have any, he said, 'It's very cold out there.' That was an understatement. When the icy blast hit me, my ears felt as though they were being burnt off as I ran for the nearest hotel to escape. It was -19 degrees, but a special cold, they said, as it came off the Great Lakes.

North Atlantic Ferry Command HQ was at the Montreal airport, Dorval, just outside the city. There the Air Commodore, an old airline pilot who looked as though he had never had it so good, told me that I would have to wait for a Mosquito to come from Toronto and in the meantime I had better arrange to go down to see the factory. He said they were arranging for an American fuel consumption expert to come and do tests around Canada with me.

In Toronto they made me very welcome, gave me a tour of the production plant and took lots of publicity pictures with their prettiest female workers pretending to help me with the difficult tasks they performed.

Whilst in Toronto, I took the opportunity to look up Murray

Mitchell's parents, as I had promised Mitch I would do if I got the opportunity. Mitch's father was a Methodist minister in the city and having telephoned Mrs Mitchell, I went around in the evening and in due course we sat down to have a cup of tea. Well, what should you really say when you are there? I decided to describe to them the sort of life we lived in the mess and told them about some of Mitch's exploits in the air. I started by asking if he had got his DFC yet. I had written the citation for it along with quite a number of others in my flight during my last week or two there, so I thought it should have come through by now. Rather casually, I thought, they said he had written to tell them, but clearly this was a matter of little account in their lives. After this slight setback, I launched into the type of work we did and what an inspiration and morale booster Mitch was, particularly when we arrived back in the mess after a long, arduous and maybe dangerous trip, dead tired, and Mitch would order a round of drinks for everybody. The Reverend Mitchell interrupted suddenly. 'Do you mean to tell me that Murray has taken to drink?' he exclaimed.

'Oh, well, no sir, not really, just the odd half pint to help restore all our spirits. Very necessary, you know, sir.'

Stony ground was not in it. 'I would rather that Murray had died than that he should have succumbed to mortal sin,' his father said. Shaken to the core, I left the household as soon as I decently could. The Reverend Mitchell had his wish; Murray got back to Canada in due course and flew into some mountains in Upper New York State, killing himself. I hope it stuck in that dreadful God-botherer's gullet for the rest of his life.

Back in Montreal, there was little to do and one week dragged into another as I waited for the Mosquito to arrive. Eventually, my American fuel expert came. A day or so later he rang me from the aerodrome. 'The plane's just landed. Its eleven o'clock now, so if you could get up here in a half hour we could do a few circuits and landings and then I could spend the afternoon on my own, familiarizing myself with it. Then we'll be ready to start the testing in the morning.' I was delighted, and was at Dorval thirty minutes later. There, out on the tarmac was the brand new Mosquito. We equipped ourselves with parachutes and climbed into the plane. Despite the cold, the engines were still warm, so we started up, checked the magneto tolerances, which was all the routine procedure necessary for in-line engines when the plane had already been flown that day.

I taxied out to the easterly end of the main runway, got take-off clearance from the control tower, and, a moment later let the brakes off and started down the runway. Here the normal procedure was to accelerate, a certain way, checking that the instruments were recording correctly, then to push the throttles open to the take-off stop on the housing, but now looking out of the aircraft and concentrating on the flying itself.

The moment I opened up the throttles to take-off position, it felt as if a mule had kicked us in the back; the plane shot forward with enormous acceleration. I could not believe it and looked down, as did my companion. To my horror, the gauges were registering idling turn-over, as though we were still on the ground taxiing. But we were not; we were hurtling into the air at a great speed, climbing steeply, already at 300 feet past the control tower, only half the way down the runway. I was not certain what to do. The instruments read that we had no engine power on at all, yet here we were rocketing up and on. My companion said, 'I wouldn't touch a thing.' I agreed. Then, with a great bang, the reduction gear on the port engine failed and the propeller itself screamed up to 6,000 rpm, with a most dreadful whine, which in fact broke my eardrums, although I did not know it then. The starboard engine reacted differently. The piston connecting rods broke through into the oil sump and the engine burst into flames.

We were not high enough to turn back to the runway. I cut both engines off, turned off the fuel supply and looked to see where I could put her down straight ahead. There were fields deep in snow, with only fence tops protruding out of them. Unfortunately we were still in an urban area and there was nowhere to land where there was comfortable room before we met houses. I chose the best I could find, and we glided down to it to crash land as near the start as possible. As we drew close I suddenly saw a nasty spindly little tree right in front of us that until that moment had been silhouetted against a hedge top.

I knew it would be fatal to try to turn the aeroplane to avoid it. Crash landings have to be made with the plane perfectly level, otherwise everybody is killed, so I had to go through it and hope to knock it down. It did not look very strong anyway. I decided that the strongest part of the plane to hit it with would be as near to the outside of the port engine as possible, and that is what we did.

The tree was in fact a lot stronger than the wing; it only lost a bit of bark, while the wing was amputated, clean as a whistle. The plane dropped like a stone into the snow and broke in half behind the cabin. The front part then proceeded to turn around and slither along in the snow for several hundred yards. The tail part, obviously not wishing to be left behind, came along too, going straight ahead, and finished tucked in against the front part, exactly where the wing had disappeared from.

The two of us scrambled out through the emergency exit above the cockpit with great alacrity, and we looked at it, waiting to see if it was going to explode or catch fire. It did not and my companion said 'thank goodness. I can go back in and get my overcoat.' He had a couple of hundred dollars in it.

Presently, a policeman arrived from an adjacent road. Leaving his bicycle against a hedge, he walked over. Looking at me, he said, 'Don't touch your left ear, it'll fall off, for sure. It's completely frozen, opaque, you know.' So it was. Eventually, an ambulance from the aerodrome arrived, picked us up and took us back to flying control.

An hour later, the Air Commodore sent for me. 'Do you realise you have just written off twenty five thousand pounds' worth of aeroplane?' He started. 'Sir,' I protested, 'that aeroplane has been tampered with, it has been sabotaged.' We had worked out by then what had happened. Between the time the plane had landed that morning and the time we had arrived, mechanics had been able to open a side panel on each engine and tape down the throttle arms in the engine housings, so that they became straight-through throttles which would open up to the distance they were designed to go to at over 20,000 feet when their anaroid mechanism had fully expanded them as the air pressure fell away. It was very simple; it meant that instead of opening the engines up to a boost power of 9 lb, I actually opened them to over 20 lb and the dial hands had gone right around the clock to the position where they would be when idling on the ground.

When I told him what we had figured out, the Air Commodore agreed. 'But you broke the rules,' he said. All engines are supposed to be run up fully before any plane leaves the tarmac here on all occasions. If you had done that, this might not have happened.'

'Excuse me, sir,' I retorted, 'that is standard procedure for all radial engines, which is what every plane that comes through here is equipped with. But this plane has in-line engines, and the engine bearers cannot take the strain of frequent running up on the ground, which is why they are run up only once a day.'

'You have seen the regulations here,' he said. 'In fact you must have signed that you had read them, so I shall order Red Endorsement on your log-book and you will return to England by the first aeroplane that can take you tomorrow.' With that, he started to dismiss me.

'Just before I go, sir,' I said, 'I have been fighting the war in England for the past five years. If I can get a job in Washington, where I know they are short of people because nobody is being allowed out of Britain now with the invasion of Europe pending, would you object?'

'You can have till eleven o'clock tomorrow. If you can get a posting in that time, you may go. Otherwise, definitely not. This cannot be allowed to develop into a political incident. We're having enough trouble with the French Canadians already, and I want you a long way away. There will be no enquiry. You have simply crashed the aircraft on take-off.'

I knew Sir Vivian Gabriel in the RAF delegation in Washington. What his role was I did not know, but often when I went to London he was enjoying my family's hospitality at our flat and I reckoned he owed the Braithwaites something. Luckily, I was able to contact him immediately and at 10.00 the following morning, a signal came through posting me to the RAF delegation. That evening, I had to present my log book to Wing Commander Anderson, to have it endorsed. He filled in the necessary form, then handed it to me. 'I'm not putting this in your log-book, Flight Lieutenant. We all know what happened and the Air Commodore is just shit-scared that his security is so bad that this could have been done in broad daylight in front of all our noses.' He suggested something rude that I might prefer to do with the endorsement certificate, and wished me luck.

'Do you happen to know why this should have been done to my aircraft, sir?' I asked, sensing that he knew a lot more about it than I was ever going to.

'Did you ever hear about the *Surcouf*?' he asked.

'Why yes,' I said, 'the largest submarine in the world, 2,000 tons, built by the French before the war. What has that to do with it?'

'Well, after our fight with the French fleet at Dakar, when the French had capitulated to the Germans, some stayed capitulated and some decided to join the Allies. The *Surcouf* was one French ship that decided to come with us, and she sailed over to Halifax. This was almost three years ago, and since then she's been based at Halifax doing convoy escort duties across the Atlantic. It's only recently that we have discovered that after picking up convoy instructions in Halifax she has been going out to sea regularly and sinking our own ships. It has nothing to do with the Germans, of course. It's just that they clearly decided that the opportunity presented itself to further the French Canadian independence cause. There was nothing to do about it, but *Surcouf* conveniently went missing on her way to the Panama Canal. We are not likely to hear of it again and there were no survivors. I'm afraid your misfortune is probably in retaliation for that.'

The next day I was on my own once more, this time to Washington DC by train, still working out in my own mind what had happened. Clearly the long delay for a Mosquito to come from Toronto, when I had seen plenty there when I had made my visit, was all so that the right mechanics could be organised to have tarmac duty on the morning when my aircraft would arrive. Somebody at Toronto had obviously known a lot about our operating procedure, so that they could predict what would happen. What they were clearly unable to do was to doctor the plane at the Toronto end as they could not organise their pilot for the flight across to Montreal. I now remembered that when I had been in Toronto I had told them I would like to go down there myself to look it over before it came and then fly it back to Dorval myself, but, that was not possible; the delivery and handover to the RAF at Dorval had to be done by them. That was routine. They had their own factory delivery pilots.

At the RAF delegation I was ushered into the office of Group Captain Speight, Director of Training. In a short time he had issued me with a travel warrant to proceed to Orlando, Florida, to join an observer unit there under Group Captain Teddy

Donaldson, which was attached to a quite extraordinary American tactical unit, which had quantities of every enemy aircraft in the world that mattered. Messerschmits of all types, Focke Wulfs and Zeros. If the enemy in any theatre tried out a new tactic, such as when the Germans started firing rockets from long range on the Fortresses and Liberator formations, or bombing them from above, several crews from the action would be flown direct from the battle zone to Orlando. Having slept all the way, they would be fresh enough the following morning to brief Orlando on what had happened, and Orlando would be able to repeat the exact tactic in the skies over Florida that afternoon. Having found the best antidote, a number of new crews would be flown immediately back to the battle zone, and arriving fresh from sleep on the way, would be able to instruct the squadrons on the counter-tactics to be adopted.

The small RAF unit was there to observe and, where we could, to advise from our own operational experience. For this reason, we had a number from each command, eight in all, including the commanding officer and adjutant.

Although it was scarcely the end of March, I alighted from the train to a world garlanded in hibiscus, oleander and bougainvillea. The Adjutant met me and ushered me into the station car. Passing a golf course, he said, 'That's Squadron Leader Bartley.' Across the grass came Tony, an old school colleague of mine, who had a DFC and Bar from the Battle of Britain, arm in arm with an enchanting woman.

On my fourth day there, to my great disappointment, the unit was disbanded and I found myself on the overnight train back to Washington in company with Tony Bartley.

In Washington they could not think what to do with either of us, and ordered us to New York to await further orders. Our billet in New York was a rather seemy downtown hotel with cracked washbasins and spiders. It was called the Knicker-bocker. I went there, but my friend knew New York better, and the next time I saw him, a year and a half later, he explained that another mutual school friend of ours who lived in New York was fighting in the Pacific, and Tony had therefore being doing his duty by looking after his wife whilst there.

Eventually, Washington ordered me to return, and I was assigned a temporary task, to accompany an air vice marshal as his ADC on an official visit to Oklahoma. Our party consisted of the air vice-marshal, an Air Commodore Blackford and several others. At Miami, Oklahoma, where we had a training school, we were met by the Commanding Officer, who started telling us about the place as we drove to the aerodrome. 'Do you see those three old codgers all sitting there on the steps of that shack on the right?' They had tatty old hats and were smoking corn-cob pipes. 'They're all multi-millionaires. There's oil in these 'ere parts.' That was about the only thing worth remembering about the trip, apart from two parties and a wings parade. When we got back the air vice-marshal instructed me to write up his official report. Clearly, I did not have the making of an ADC. He was furious about my discourse on weatherbeaten, ragged multi-millionaires, and tore it up and did it again himself.

Air Commodore Blackford, however, was interesting. 'I've just been up to Montreal to investigate your crash there,' he told me. 'I am the officer in charge of all suspected sabotage. There are very few really; I have only proved six positively and two of them are yours!' I was astonished. 'Do you remember that when you were commanding the Met. Squadron in Bircham Newton a Blenheim doing the Rhombus flight couldn't get airborne one morning? It didn't crash, as it managed to stop in time.' Frankly, I could not remember, but I could well believe it, as Group used to send us some quite dreadful second-hand Blenheims, Hudsons, Albermarles, even a Flying Fortress. With the number of engine failures at different times, the fact that we could not even get one into the air on one occasion was not great surprise. 'Well,' he went on, 'it was examined and it was found that overnight all the sparking plugs, thirty-two of them in all, had been loosened – luckily too far to enable the plane to get up to take-off speed. We got the chap. He was on sentry duty and it turned out that he tried to do that sort of thing quite frequently when he got the opportunity. But, of course, we never let on to the flying personnel that this sort of thing has happened, as it would just give them something else to worry about.' He also confirmed to me what I had been told at Montreal.

Not long after this, Group Captain Speight told me that I could choose between three jobs: Embarkation Officer, Miami, Florida; VIP Reception Officer, New York; or RAF Liaison Officer to the US Air Force Training Command HQ, Fort Worth,

Texas. The latter carried $5,000 per year in additional entertainment allowances, the upgrading of my squadron leader's pay to that of a major in the US Air Force and my own long-range Harvard AT 6 to get about the country in. I did not have difficulty choosing.

Speight took me over to the big wall map on the other side of his office. 'This is Texas down here,' he said, pointing to an enormous patch of brown, 'and nobody from the delegation has ever been there, so you'll be breaking new ground. But you will find it's dreadfully hot at this time of year.' As I was about to get up to leave, I noticed a small heap of cards on his desk. They read: 'This is to certify that . . . . stationed at . . . . holds the equivalent rating in the Royal Air Force of a command pilot. Signed Director of Training, RAF Delegation.'

'Do you think I might have one of those, sir?' I asked.

'Don't see why not,' replied Speight, and with that he filled in my name and HQ Training Command, signed it and put the official RAF stamp on it.

I had to have a car, and an aunt in Georgia told me I could have her son's Dodge convertible for $300 as he was fighting in the Pacific. I therefore took a train from Washington to Augusta, and then set off by car on the long journey to Forth Worth, Texas.

I immediately noticed a frequent road sign. On a white square was the word 'WAR' and underneath it, '30'. Cars were driving at at least 50 mph, often considerably more, and when I tried to go at 30 mph I was abused for holding everybody up. I was therefore soon going along with the rest of the traffic. After a day, when I was in the middle of Alabama, a police car drew up with its sirens screaming. 'You were driving at sixty miles an hour when the speed limit is thirty,' said the officer.

'Well, officer,' I replied, 'I was not quite sure what those signs meant, as I haven't seen a car in a day that paid any attention to them, and I have never driven a car in the USA until yesterday.'

'Where you from then?' he asked. I was wearing RAF uniform, but that obviously meant nothing to him. I told him I was a British officer in the British Royal Air Force. 'Does that mean you're a soldier?' he asked, looking suspiciously at me.

'No officer, I'm not a soldier, I'm an airman.'

That confused him more than ever as he knew that America had soldiers in its air force. 'Well, you'll have to follow me to the court house, son, and I'll just have to charge you,' he said, at the same time flagging down another vehicle and telling it to slow down. One arrest was clearly enough to handle at one time.

In due course we started down the road, luckily in the direction I was going anyway. By the time we had reached the court house, about 8 miles on, at exactly 30 mph, we must have had sixty cars behind us, as he was not letting anybody go past. Eventually I followed him off the road onto a dusty forecourt with a broken-down frame-built shack that stood behind two old petrol pumps.

In here,' he said, and I followed him in. There was a very ancient rusty Coca Cola bin the sort that you had to lift the whole four-foot lid to reach the contents, and behind, messing about with some merchandise on shelves was a little old woman, with a face, neck and hands as weather-beaten and wrinkled as a black walnut out of its shell on the Christmas dinner table.

The officer did not seem to be doing anything about going to fetch the judge he said would be trying me. The time went by and periodically I repeated that I was going to Fort Worth which was a long way away and I was in a hurry. He just answered that the judge would be along in a few minutes. Nothing else was said; he didn't address a word to the old woman who was still scratching around at her shelves, nor she to him.

Eventually, after what seemed an eternity, the woman pulled herself up behind the Coca Cola bin, produced a wooden gavel from behind it, and hit the top of it an enormous clout. 'Court in session,' she announced in a loud voice. 'Officer, I sees you have arrested this here man. What is the charge?'

'Speeding on Highway 80 East at sixty miles per hour, Your Honour,' said the officer.

'What's he do?' asked the judge.

'Don't really know for sure, your Honour. Says he's a soldier, but I never see no uniform like that before.' Then to me,

'Is you really a soldier, boy? Didn't seem too sure on the road back there, and it does make a difference to the court.'

'Yes,' I replied, now quite resigned to being classified as a soldier.

'How y'ar plead?' Asked the woman.

I had already decided no articulate defence on my part would do any good at all, in fact would probably make matters worse. 'Guilty, your Honour.' I replied.

'Thirty dollars fine and five dollars costs,' she said.

'Good heavens, I haven't that sort of money. I've only just arrived in your country and I have fifty dollars on me. If you want that amount I won't be able to get to Fort Worth, so quite probably you'll have to put me in jail.'

'What y'er going to Fort Worth to do?' asked the officer.

'I'm reporting to the US Army Air Force Headquarters there, where I have to take up my assignment, and I'm now going to be late anyway.'

'Judge, maybe as he really is a soldier, you are being a bit hard.' They muttered together, then the woman said, 'Court has reconsidered. Fine reduced to ten dollars and five dollars costs.'

That was a relief, but it was not the end of it. We had to have an arrest ticket and a receipt, and they could both only write very slowly. Moreover, they came to a grinding halt over words like 'delegation' and 'Royal Air Force''. It was eventually done, I paid over the money which went with another great clang into the Coca Cola bin, and out I stepped into the sunshine accompanied by the officer. As I went to get into the car, he came across. 'Now, look, son,' he said, 'I can see as you're in a hurry, so I'll tell you. You won't see another patrol car like mine short of the state line this afternoon, but if you do it'll look like this one. When you gets to Louisiana, they're coloured white with blue stripes, and about the same in Mississippi, then after Shreveport when you get into Texas they'll be green with white. You can go as fast as you like, but keep looking. If you do you won't get caught again. Now, that's good advice boy, and worth the fifteen dollars it's cost you to get it. Good luck.'

The Texas and Pacific (T & P) Building in Fort Worth housed about 6,000 personnel including no less than five generals of varying seniority. I had to report to a colonel. 'How very nice to meet you, Squadron Leader, I'll take you down the corridor to the office we have chosen for you.' He led me some twenty yards or so down a corridor to an office in which I could have parked a small aeroplane. There was a vast desk in the middle opposite the usual map of the USA. 'Do you think you'll be comfortable here, Squadron Leader?' he asked.

I was still looking around in amazement, when he added. 'And

This photograph was taken after 'D' Donald's 150th sortie over enemy territory. It went on to complete many more sorties and then went on a goodwill tour of America. On VE Day the aircraft crashed at Calgary, killing both Flight Lieutenant Briggs, DSO, DFC, DFM and Flying Officer Bates, DFC.

Mosquito 'D' Donald of 1409 Flight, seen when well overdue and just prior to landing with one engine US.

No. 139 Squadron (Bennet's Private Air Force) on 30 January 1944. The Author is seated front row 4th from the left.

Wyton, January 18th 1944, on the occasion of George Hodder's award of the DFC. He is seen second from the left. Seen extreme left is the No. 1 Fitter, Joe Gardner, third from left the Author and then 'Nocker' Elms, the Rigger

Mosquito IV DZ/359, 'R' Robert. This is the Author's favourite aircraft and he first flew it on 1 November 1942, when it was 'S' Sugar. She captured the 'Berlin and Back' record on 8 October 1943, with the Author at the controls in a time of three hours and fifty-five minutes.

When taking off from Dorval in Canada, on the test flight of a new Mosquito that was delivered for a record-breaking flight, the engine automatic boost controls failed simultaneously on both engines. The aircraft rocketed from 90 mph to 170 mph in a few hundred yards before the constant speed mechanism failed on the port engine and the starboard engine burst into flames. The Author was forced to crash land the aircraft and hit the tree which cut the starboard wing clean off the aircraft. Both pilot and navigator escaped unhurt and sabotage was the suspected cause of the incident.

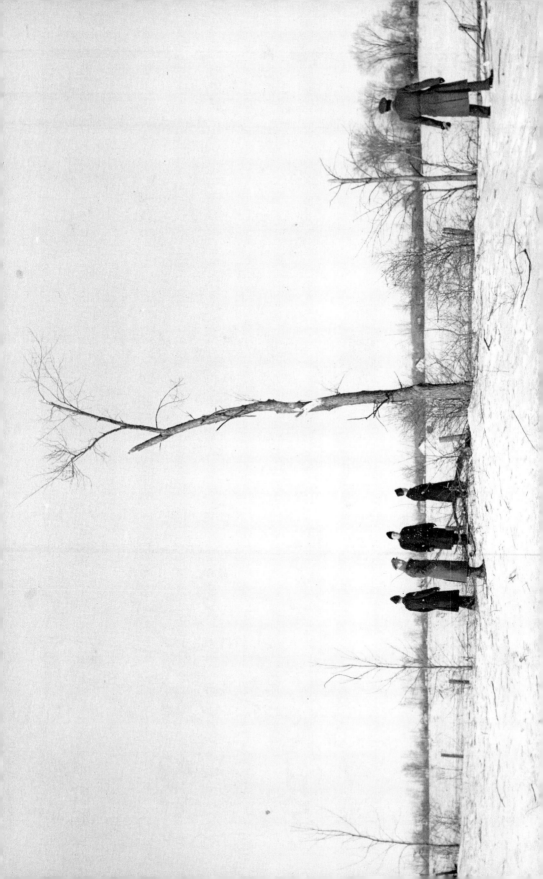

The Author in
his 83rd year.

Caricatures of some of the personalities at the School of General
Reconnaissance, Squires Gate.

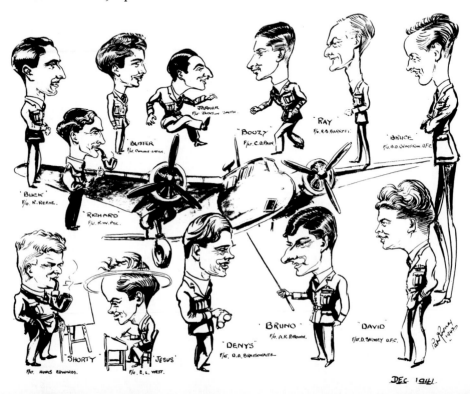

I have chosen six secretaries for you.' That was too much for me; I thought he expected me to have work for six secretaries whereas I was to choose one from the six. Nevertheless, I did not think I could cope with this. 'Colonel, sir, would you by any possible chance have an office, somewhat smaller and nearer your own,' I said. 'Then if your own secretary just has a little time occasionally could I borrow her to deal with my office work?'

Since that seemed to present no problem, I thought we had better get down to business. 'Colonel,' I said, 'I understand this appointment was requested by you not by us. Can you tell me what I am meant to do?'

'I don't really know all about it myself,' replied the colonel, 'but I think it's due to the RAF having four flying schools here, with mixed staff: the flying instructors are yours and the ground staff, medical officers and so on, are ours. I think your job is to be on hand in case anything goes wrong. Also, you will have an AT 6 to go around the country in and you might like to fit into your agenda visits to some of our training establishments, where I am sure we will have some training methods that you will probably not have encountered in Europe. With this in mind I have prepared an authorisation for you to fly any aircraft at any of our bases with the consent of the commanding officer.'

This was all too good to be true, but there was more. The public relations staff arranged my accommodation for me and also informed me that I was now an honorary member of the leading country club in the area. There really was almost nothing to complain about in my new situation. One problem was that I had to take four large water bottles from the refrigerator to bed with me: one for drinking, one for pouring all over the sheets before I got in and two for topping up during the night. Texas really is hot in the summer, but, with a supply of cold water bottles, it became quite bearable. My other problem was that I never adjusted to the correct protocol for addressing people. There were six large lifts in the T& P Building, and everybody started work at 8.30. There were five generals and it was odds on that I would arrive in an elevator with one of them, who would exclaim loudly, 'Good morning, sir.' How does a lowly squadron leader address a general when the latter has started the ball rolling with 'sir?' I generally replied, 'Good morning, general', which seemed to get by.

I was advised that my RAF uniform was quite unfit for the climate and also that British tropical kit was inappropriate, as the Americans required long trousers to be worn, while we wore Bermuda shorts. So with the help of a military tailor, I managed a mixture of our uniform, with belted tunic and shoulder epaulettes, and American trousers in ultra-light tropical material, which really looked rather smart. What I did not get away with was the squadron leader pennant with which the personnel staff suddenly adorned my car. A very short telephone conversation with Group Captain Speight got rid of that.

Our flying schools were at Miami, Oklahoma, where I had already been, Mesa Arizona, Clewiston, Florida and Terrell, Texas. Terrell was just a few miles beyond Dallas, the neighbouring city to Fort Worth. Fort Worth was a cattle town, Dallas an oil town, and the inhabitants did not mix. I got to know some super people in Fort Worth, and, through my friends at Terrell, also in Dallas. They always knew who I was talking about in the other city but they would never have spoken to them.

I started by going around our flying schools one by one, and then expanded the trips to include American training bases. When it came to visiting Clewiston, on the southern end of Lake Okechobee in south-central Florida I decided to hitch a lift across to the Bahamas from Miami for the weekend as I had a lot of friends there. It was a splendid couple of days and I bought a lot of sporting equipment and such like from our NAAFI stores, as that was so much cheaper than the American PX in Fort Worth. On the Monday I returned and flew to spend a night with my relatives in Georgia, from where my visit to Craig Field, Selma, Alabama for the next morning was only a short flight.

I was due at Selma at 11.00, but already I had a routine worked out where I would always arrive at an American base at least five minutes early, as the Commanding Officer invariably turned out to receive his RAF visitor in person and such courtesy called for an impeccable arrival on the part of the RAF Officer.

I arrived on the circuit without any idea what to do. To my horror, there were literally hundreds of AT 6s whirling around the airfield, just like swarms of bees, except that they would regularly form up in threes on their approach and come into land in formation. I had never flown formation in my life, let

alone landed in one. Could I possibly say, 'please clear the
runway so that the RAF Liaison Officer can land?' That was
quite impossible, I must hope for a miracle, such as, 'we will
clear the runway for the RAF Liaison Officer.' But, of course that
did not happen.

At precisely 10.55 I called up. 'This is the RAF Liaison Officer.
May I have landing instructions please?' Back came the dreaded
reply: 'Royal Air Force Liaison Officer, just come in with the
others. Tack onto any formation you like.' My heart sank. But I
found an AT 6 with another chap coming in on its starboard
side, so I moved in on its port side. We went in on the approach,
with me pushing my throttle backwards and forwards trying to
keep some semblance of position. Down we came to the runway,
200 yards behind the formation in front and 200 yards in front of
the formation behind.

Then clearly I got it wrong. I was so busy trying to ensure that
I did not run into the wing of the plane 20 feet ahead of me and
just to my right that I suppose I stalled. I certainly broke both
wings, the propeller and the tail wheel!

The formation behind managed a Prince of Wales' feathers to
climb away from the scene. Looking and feeling like a real
Charlie, I stopped just on the grass to the left of the runway, and
I could hear loudspeakers in all directions yelling, 'Clear the 170
runway, crash on 170 runway,' and then repeating it until the
swarm of AT 6s had gone somewhere else. What was just as bad
was counting the number of vehicles approaching me as I sat in
the cockpit. There were seventeen: fire tenders, ambulances,
trucks with cranes, a photographic van, and last of all, the car
with a flag identifying it as the general's car.

I was half out of the cockpit when the general, driving
himself, pulled up beside me. He looked a bit surprised, because
I was still in Bermuda shorts and stockings, standard wear in the
Bahamas, but as I have said, not in the US forces. I must have
looked and certainly felt – very stupid.

'Small errors can happen, Squadron Leader,' said the general.
'Think nothing of it. You undoubtedly need a drink. We can
leave this,' waving his arm vaguely at my AT 6. 'They'll have it
cleared away in no time.'

'Excuse me, sir,' I said, 'thank you very much, but do you
mind if I get my baggage first?'

'Of course, I wasn't thinking. I'll help you.' I opened the side panel and passed out my kit bag to my high-ranking porter. 'OK,' he said, 'now let's get away,'

'No, sir, there's more to come yet.' Out came a tennis racquet and a dozen tennis balls. These the general stowed away in the car and went to shut it up.

'Sorry, sir, but there's one more thing.' And, with that I dug out of the bottom of the luggage compartment a case of White Horse whisky.

We got in the car and started back to the buildings. 'Well, Squadron Leader,' he said, 'this has been quite an eventful morning for us both, but I know just how to settle it all up. You have – quite unavoidably, of course – disrupted my training programme, the payment for which is that we will drink the case of whisky before you depart. Oh, also, there is another condition. So long as you are on my station you will remain dressed as you are now.'

Throwing a packet of Chesterfields and a book of matches over to me, he said, 'I think we both need a cigarette.'

'I don't smoke, sir, but I'll light one for you.' I knocked a cigarette out of the pack, passed it to him, and, leaning over struck a match. I did it wrong, and the whole pack exploded and dropped right in his lap. Luckily, the general had pretty good reactions. There did not seem to be any damage done at all.

Eventually, we reached his office and he called in his private secretary. I began to feel noticeably better, as she was the most beautiful girl I had ever seen in my life. 'Louise,' said the general, 'you'll be helping entertain the squadron leader during his stay here. I hope you won't mind, but I have insisted on the short trousers as long as he stays.' Louise did not seem to mind the assignment or the shorts, so life was improving. The general asked her to get Colonel Wilkinson.

Colonel Wilkinson turned out to be the Chief Engineer Officer. 'Colonel, there has been a mishap with the squadron leader's aeroplane on the 170 runway. Please have a look at it and come back within the half-hour if you can with a report on why it had to crash.'

Thirty minutes later, colonel Wilkinson was back. 'There was absolutely nothing the squadron leader could have done about it, sir.' The tail wheel was locked hard over before he landed and he had no chance whatever.'

We had two splendid days and evenings at Selma, and when I had to get back to Fort Worth, the general said, 'I've been thinking about this. Your plane is now on the scrap-heap, and I have about ten thousand of them between here and Montgomery, next door. Would you like to take one and bring it back at your convenience? Or would you prefer to take one of my pilots over with you to bring it back? Or, perhaps you would like to take your pick of what we have and you can keep it till the end of the war. Nobody will ever miss it!'

I voted for the first, as I really did not think it was fair, after all the trouble I had caused, to take an aeroplane from them as well. Moreover, I was thinking, how nice it would be to see more of Louise.

'When are you proposing to go, Denys?' he asked.

'I was thinking of first thing in the morning, sir.'

'That's not a bad idea,' he replied. 'I have to go over to Shreveport, so maybe we could fly together.'

'So long as it's not formation, sir.'

'OK, we'll meet up in the Operations Room at seven thirty so that we can get a good start.'

At 7.00, I was up with all my gear stowed away in the plane assigned to me, and by 7.30 I had completed the Operations Room form and walked over to the desk. The General came up from the other side. I laid my form down, signed it and put my cross in the 'Command Pilot' slot, produced my RAF Delegation card, and passed them over to the controller. 'That's OK,' said the controller signing it. In fact he could not do anything else. Command pilots, almost always generals with over 20,000 hours' flying experience do not need authorisation from any controller; they can fly when and where they like.

The general passed his sheet over, signed it and put his cross in the Senior Pilot's slot. The controller said, 'Sorry, sir, I can't sign you out. The weather's perfect here but there are thunderstorms between here and your destination.' I had 1,500 hours' flying time and he had 15,000 but senior pilots did not have the same clout as Command Pilots.

One of my next trips was to our school at Mesa, Arizona, and when I told the Wing Commander there that I was going on to make a quick visit to an American air base in California, he asked if he could come too. As we were returning the same day, it was another early start. At that time of the morning we could not get a weather report from the west coast, but the outlook seemed perfect where we were. Just before the Rockies, we came to the last check-out station, and we asked there for the weather at our destination. Again, it could not be provided. This was the point of no return, but we both agreed that the sun always shines in California, so on we went.

We crossed the Rockies and, to our dismay, saw nothing but a sea of solid cloud below and ahead of us. We were able to skid down the side of the mountains, eventually reaching the plains below, where we flew in real Met. Flight bad visibility until we ran across an aerodrome called El Torro, at which we landed. It was an American naval field and they thought we were quite mad. We managed just a couple of hours at my official call, and then flew back in the afternoon to the more reliable weather of Arizona, with promises to return when they were able to give us a good weather forecast beforehand.

The next time I was in California, I again had to leave immediately. There was a telegraph waiting for me there from Group Captain Speight to say I was to go to Terrel, our school near Dallas, the following Thursday to make arrangements for guess who, my old Air Vice-Marshal who was to give out the wings at the passing-out parade on the Saturday. My little aeroplane did not fly very fast, so I only just made Fort Worth by the Thursday evening.

Terrel was a civilian airport belonging to a Colonel Long, a swashbuckling figure of great character. The first thing I had to do was to locate him. 'That's all right, young man,' he said, 'everything's under control. I just want to know what your Air Vice-Marshal is like, what his dislikes and likes are. I have a reputation as a good host, and that sort of information is always vital. Ring me back in the morning when you have found out.'

I rang Speight in Washington, and it turned out that the Air-Vice-Marshal was a man of simple taste: blonde women, white chargers and champagne. He had spent his entire service career in the Middle East, where presumably these three prerequisitions were more readily available as a complete menu than in England. 'Right, that's fine,' said Colonel Long. 'He's booked into the Presidential Suite at the Adolphus Hotel, but I'm paying all expenses, so nobody need worry. You just see that he meets the dignitaries when he lands, and that they all set off in time to get to the luncheon at Terrel field before the parade.'

Everything went splendidly. As the Air Vice-Marshal descended the steps of the 8.00 Delta flight from Washington, there were a couple of photographers on hand. He took off his white gloves as he came down, stroked his distinguished white moustache with the back of one hand, first one way and then the other, and handed me the white gloves. The Mayor and Mayoress of Dallas were introduced to him by the Airport Manager and presently the cars swept out of the aerodrome to Terrel, Texas with me following in my little Dodge convertible.

The luncheon and parade passed off well, with only two cadets fainting in the Texas heat, and at 4.00 it was time to take the Air Vice-Marshal to the Adolphus Hotel. I had gone ahead and got his baggage into his room. The Mayor and Mayoress delivered him to the main entrance, and, feeling like a brilliant and reliable ADC, I delivered him to the Presidential Suite. Here, however, I made what I afterwards saw was a foolish error. 'I hope this is alright for you, sir,' I said. 'Only $150, a night. I presume that was all right.' The Air Vice-Marshal turned slightly puce. 'Sorry, sir, that was only a joke. Colonel Long, your host, booked this and told me to tell you he is paying for everything.' I beat a hasty retreat, with instructions to be on time and return to escort him to the Baker Hotel for Colonel Long's grand dinner.

There were fifty of us at dinner, with the Air Vice-Marshal, a very exotic blonde on his left, and Colonel Long's main party, all at the head of the table. I naturally was a long way away, at the very bottom of the table. At 11.00 knowing that I was to put the Air Vice-Marshal on the 11.30 Delta flight the next morning, I went up to the Air Vice-Marshal and asked to excuse myself – all very proper and accepted. I left him with the blonde on one knee, and a glass of champagne precariously balanced in his free hand.

At 9.00 the next day, Sunday, I presented myself at the Adolphus. There was no Air Vice-Marshal. I went to the Presidential Suite, to find it being cleaned out. There was no baggage anywhere, they said. I rang Speight in panic. He made enquiries and instructed me to look in every barber's shop and coffee shop in town, as he had been known to frequent such places. I drew a blank. I got in the Dodge and went to the airport. He was not there. I returned to the Adolphus – no sign of him. I returned again to the airport. The plane had now landed and would leave in a half hour. At 11.30 they took on board the last passengers, and started the engines. I turned away. I had genuinely lost my Air Vice-Marshal.

The following day, Speight rang me to say that I was to be replaced immediately. The Air Vice-Marshal had in fact caught the plane with or without his white gloves. Oh, that I had known what a thorough man that Colonel Long was. The blonde turned out to be a breeder of white chargers! She had taken him out to her ranch that night and they had been for a ride that morning. He was therefore late for the plane's scheduled departure, but someone had used their influence to have it held back at the last moment. There was, I was told, a terrific argument about the matter in Washington, but eventually a Squadron Leader came to replace me. He was Briggs, known as Bismarck Briggs because he was the pilot of the Catalina flying boat that found the *Bismarck* the day it was sunk. The whole hull of his flying boat had been shot away, so that it sank immediately on landing, but he stayed with the *Bismarck* for about sixteen hours, directing warships and aircraft to where she was, so that they could sink her.

I was given a month to show Briggs around and introduce him to my many contacts, but as it turned out I was delighted at the turn of events. Leonard Slee, my old Pathfinder group captain, was now in the Arakan coastal strip of Burma and had a wing of Kitty Hawks. He wanted to know if I wanted the wing commander vacancy? Various people were going from Pathfinders and the elephant shooting was spectacular. I could not wait. I had had enough of America by then. I was fully refreshed and had begun to notice that the only parties I liked were the ones where aircrews were off to operational flying, generally in the Pacific. Most people took the same view; we were still fighting a war, and there was none in Texas.

Briggs seemed to settle in well, although immediately after I handed over he landed his AT 6 downwind and smashed it. Perhaps it was because boat pilots usually have a generous stretch of water to land on. Later he put his shoes on one morning in Arizona without shaking them out first. Scorpions like the warmth of a boot or shoe to crawl into overnight, and he was bitten. He got phlebitis and spent some time in hospital. He was better off, though, than another man we slightly knew there. He sat on a lavatory seat and was bitten somewhere most unfortunate by a black widow spider; he died in agony.

Instead of sending me back to England, or even straight to India, the Air Vice-Marshal played a last wicked little card: the Bahamas. I was to command a flight of training Liberators. Under no circumstances were personnel allowed to visit the USA, so I felt in rather the same position as the Duke of Windsor, exiled. I told a tall story about not being able to fly in the glare of the sun on a tropical sea and the risk of killing people. Somebody else wanted the flight I had been given anyway, so I was attached to headquarters staff whilst we saw off a rather vicious hurricane which caused the evacuation of all RAF planes and aircrew to Cuba and Florida. After this, I was told to go to Moncton in Canada to await passage by boat to England. In Miami, the embarkation officer altered my orders, gave me two weeks' leave and instructions to catch the *Queen Mary* from New York on 12 October.

CHAPTER EIGHT

45 Squadron

Back in London once again who should be waiting for me to phone him but my guardian angel, Phil Hazleman. 'What do you want to do now?' he asked.

'I want to go to India, Phil.'

'Please think twice about that. It's a long way away and I can't send you out as a wing commander. In fact, you would have to go as a flight lieutenant. I have another idea. Your old met. Squadron, 521, is presently without a CO. It is still at Bircham Newton. Wouldn't it be a good idea to put the clock back several years?'

A week after I arrived back at Bircham Newton, in November 1944, the whole unit was posted to Langham, an aerodrome along the coast on high cliffs looking over the North Sea, and exposed to the icy blast of winds direct from the Arctic. At Bircham Newton there had been a great commanding officer; at Langham, there was not. His name was Clauston and he had many decorations to prove his bravery, amongst which was an AFC from before the war for testing the strength of barrage balloon cables by flying a Fairey Battle into them and spinning off them. That had supplemented his pay by £20 a cable. As a station commander however, he was a shocker. There were two Fleet Air Arm Buccaneer squadrons there, and now the met. Squadron arrived – no Mosquitoes now, just Hurricanes, Gladiators and whatever Rhombus aircraft were provided at the time. To Clauston, 521 spoilt his station's operational image. All ground crews lived in Nissen huts, which at the best of times were perishing cold, but now the Station Commander said there was not enough coke to heat all units, the Buccaneer squadron ground crews were to have it all; 521 were to riddle that was left from their throw-outs, and try to keep warm on that.

Viscount Stansgate, DSO, DFC, the father of Tony Benn, the labour MP, was making a tour of RAF stations; the Labour Party were aware the war was coming to an end and were working up their propaganda machine. Clauston caused an order to be pinned on my squadron notice board, giving all officers a three-line whip to attend Lord Stangate's lecture. I took it down and replaced it, saying it was illegal to order any officer to attend a political meeting. I had had enough; I wrote to the Air Ministry suggesting that the man was not fit to command a station, and removed my Gladiator flight back to Bircham Newton, running the squadron from there with the minimum of visits back to the hostile territory of Langham. We were both posted, he with a promotion to air commodore in Germany, me with demotion back to flight lieutenant, but on my way at long last to the Far East.

I took a week's embarkation leave in London, where I arranged for the Royal Geographical Society to accept photographs I proposed to send back of the three great rivers that run north to south in the area I was going to. I had been given an original Leica camera that had started life going up the Congo with an explorer at the turn of the century and, armed with this, I was proposing to do my own exploring during leaves sandwiched between tiger shoots from howdahs, of course

I also bought two very large maps of India and eastward, drew lots of grids on them for map references and gave my mother written instructions on how to read the letters I would be sending, so that they would know where I was. (On my return to England I found that my parents had not understood this at all and had come to the conclusion from the way my letters read that I was going mad!)

We flew out to Karachi in a Sunderland from Poole to Djerba, Cairo, Baghdad and then to our destination. On arrival, the other passengers, who were all army or navy, were taken straight to the Palace Hotel to await onward travelling instructions. I was the only RAF officer on board, and as a flight lieutenant I was driven out to the Karachi Transit Camp in the desert. There I was guided to a tent by the most evil-looking Sikh bearer I ever saw. His bloodshot eyes stared through me. I wondered how many British Army troops had been killed by him, or at least by his father, up the Khyber Pass in days gone by.

I walked across to the mess, a vast marquee held up by stout wooden poles sticking out of the sand. All around were pilot officers, flying officers and flight lieutenants, who seemed greener the more I got accustomed to them. I listened to the tanoy calling people to the Accounts Office to collect their advance pay, and the more I listened, the more I realised the vulnerable position I was in. I was on a completely strange continent; nobody knew me, and it was just possible that I might be sent off somewhere as a flight lieutenant and never be heard of again. I got up and walked out to my tent. Quickly I opened up my bags to find my squadron leader epaulettes, and in a moment I had substituted them for the flight lieutenant's stripes. Back in the marquee, I did not have to wait long for the tanoy to call out, 'Flight Lieutenant Braithwaite next.' In the Accounts Office the pilot officer accountant, with his face in his figures, said 'Flight Lieutenant Braithwaite, you are entitled to six hundred rupees advance pay.' As he pushed the paper across his desk for me to sign, he looked up, saw I was a squadron leader and leapt to his feet in astonishment, saluting, at the same time. 'I'm dreadfully sorry, sir. We had you down as a flight lieutenant. You are entitled to seventeen hundred rupees advance pay which I will arrange immediately. But, sir, you shouldn't be here at all. You should be in the Palace Hotel where all the senior officers go. I'll arrange transport for you right away and send for your bags if you will wait here, please.'

An hour later I was ensconced in considerably better accommodation in the Palace Hotel and, as much as anything I didn't have to worry about that dreadful Sikh and whether he was going to have that nastly curved knife in the middle of my back before morning. The only thing that slightly worried me was the extra 1,100 rupees they had given me. However, I felt I had some defence if I was court martialed for it. I had forgotten entirely to draw my extra expenses allowance running at $5,000 per annum while I was the RAF Liaison Officer in Fort Worth. So I decided that I had to be in credit.

Twelve days later I was flown to Calcutta aboard the Empire flying boat *Caledonia*, and a day or so later was sent for by an Air Commodore. 'What do you expect to do here, Braithwaite?'

'I've come to take up the wing commander flying position with Group Captain Leonard Slee's Kitty Hawk wing in the Arakan, Sir.'

'Oh yes, I know something about that, but first I want to look at your log-books.' I had them with me and passed them over. The Air Commodore ran through them, then said, 'When did you last fly fighters, Squadron Leader?'

'Well, sir, I haven't. I've flown Spitfires and Hurricanes, but not as fighters.'

'Have you fired guns?'

'No, Sir.'

'Well, you are a very experienced Mosquito pilot, probably more so than anybody in this theatre. I'm sorry. I know you wanted to try your hand at something else, but I'm not allowing it. I need you elsewhere. As it happens, I have a Mosquito strike squadron up country who have just lost their commanding officer. But first I'll need you to go to Group HQ at Monywa to meet Air Marshal Peake, who is coming up from Ceylon next week, to get his approval. I have already discussed this with Group Captain Slee. Very sorry to disappoint you, but the decision is final. I'll see you again when you get back from Monywa.'

Monywa turned out to be an island at the confluence of the Irrawaddy and the Chindwin rivers south-west of Mandalay. Mandalay was still in the hands of the Japanese and all the land on the opposite sides of the river from Monywa were infested with Japanese patrols. However, the rivers were broad and savage and the Japanese air force had by now almost entirely disappeared, so the island itself was quite secure.

I had a few days to wait for the arrival of the Air Marshal, but eventually he did arrive, gave me about five minutes, during which he asked me a few questions about operating experiences, and then told me to report back to the Air Commodore in Calcutta.

'Right, Braithwaite,' said the Air Commodore, 'you are to

proceed to 45 Squadron at Khumbigram in Assam, where you will find a mostly Australian Mosquito squadron. But before you leave here, you will go to the hospital at Dum Dum where you will find the previous commanding officer, Wing Commander Johnny Walker. He will brief you, and then you will go on to report to Khumbigram.'

Wing Commander Walker was lying in bed when I got to his hospital, his head all bound up; he certainly didn't look very well. 'You've got a tricky job ahead of you, Braithwaite. I took over some months ago after the first CO blew himself up at Mingladon airfield at Rangoon on his first trip. He fired at a petrol bowser and it went up as he flew over it.' Shades of Charlie Rose, I thought. 'Anyway,' he continued, 'he survived and is now a prisoner of war.'

The story was that he had been operating in the North African desert when he was approached to form the first Mosquito squadron in India. He made a deal whereby he would take all Australian air and ground crew, as far as possible, and that they would do one tour of operations, and then go on home to Australia. Many of them had been away from home for four years and had lost their wives and girlfriends. Worse still, they had all been sent white feathers received when Australia thought it was going to be invaded by the Japanese; their friends and families thought they ought to have been in their own country to defend it, rather than fighting to save England, which at that moment they did not think too much about.

The net result was that they were now a pretty hardy bunch of brigands who stopped at nothing, did not like the British much and certainly resented being commanded by a Britisher. Moreover they really were the 'lost squadron'. Nobody had thought to boost their morale with medals. Johnny Walker had fought in the Battle of Britain, without recognition, but since then had been pen-pushing in the Air Ministry and that made matters worse. He then went on to tell me lurid stories which are not confirmed in the squadron records. Even his own end is totally different in the official write-up from what he recounted to me. Nevertheless, he was clearly very brave and lost an eye and had almost been scalped when his cockpit windscreen was hit by enemy fire whilst he was attacking a bridge for the fourth time because he could not get his bombs to drop. He managed, with the help of his navigator, to get back to an aerodrome, which, with one eye out and cascades of blood pouring down his forehead into the remaining one, was quite an achievement.

'The best of luck', said Johny Walker as I left him and took myself off in the direction of Khumbigram.

The day I arrived at Khumbigram was marred by a Mosquito straight out of routine service taking off, climbing like mad for a moment, then diving straight into the jungle off the end of the runway. What rotten luck, I thought, if that was an Australian crew so near to going home after so long. It transpired the elevator controls had been connected the wrong way round. In the evening, the group captain called all crews in to discuss a reconnaissance that Group had asked for. They wanted a plane out at the Siamese border at first light, but nobody wanted to do it, simply because nobody had night-flying experience. Thinking this would be my opportunity to let these people know I was worth some respect, I offered to take the flight. The group captain refused, which was possibly just as well as he would still have had to find me a navigator. The airfield was set in a valley surrounded by some of the wickedest high mountains in the world, and, as it turned out, this was the season of forest fires which reduced visibility in the mountains to almost fog conditions on occasions.

Much to my astonishment, the following morning I found that there was somebody I knew at Khumbigram: Flight Lieutenant Bamford, whom I had known years before at Squires Gate, Blackpool, when I had driven him out to that Botha. He was popular with the Squadron and undoubtedly gave me support among people to whom I was an unknown stranger who unlike these unlucky souls, had been awarded two DFCs whilst they all had none, although they had probably done just as much operational flying as I had.

My first trip came after a few days: fourteen planes down the Irrawaddy to attack some buildings. 'You will lead, sir,' said the flight lieutenant.

'Of course I won't,' I replied. 'I don't know your type of operation at all. I have it all to learn. I'll go Red four if I may.' That was tail-end Charlie in flight vernacular.

'All right,' said the Flight Lieutenant, 'I'll lead.' They had found me a navigator who was supernumerary in the Squadron.

I started to fly with him, although I had already cabled Phil Hazleman telling him I needed the best navigator he could find me, as soon as possible.

We flew through narrow valleys toward the Burmese plain. To me it was sheer madness. Visibility was rotten because of the forest fires, and we could not see four Mosquitoes at one time, let alone fourteen. I reckoned that if the leader had not stayed in the centre of the valleys, he would have flown one of his flanks right into a mountainside. Furthermore, I could not understand why they did not go up to 10,000 or 12,000 feet for half an hour and fly through in clear air? The reason for that became clear later: they were trained to fly at zero feet off the ground and to fly higher than necessary was quite unthinkable.

Eventually we went down to the plain, which resembled flat expanses of the Highlands of Scotland, with scrub-like heather, but frequent clumps of oak trees. As we flew along I saw, to my horror, that all the other planes were skimming just above the ground through the oak trees, below the branches.

'Go under the branches, sir. The Japs are very good with their small-arms fire, and we'll get hit for sure if you go over the trees,' said Flying Officer Whitcut, my navigator.

'We'll get killed if we try to go under them. I think I'll take my chances,' I replied. Sometimes, the Australians went under the branches less than 10 feet off the ground and the Mosquito's size required all of that for minimum clearance. I was to discover that every time they came back from an operation, the air intakes would be covered in heather picked up by the propeller blades. Happily, we were not fired on and in due course arrived at our target, a building that looked like a prison, with four wings protruding out from a central hub. I managed to put my bombs on the target and away we all went. Then the flight leader called me up, 'Red four, would you like to break away from the formation, proceed east until you hit the north – south railway and then turn north and photograph all the bridges up to short of Mandalay?' I was delighted to leave the formation, on which I had been keeping station for the better part of a couple of hours.

I soon picked up the railway line and began to fly northward, alongside it, at about 50 feet. As soon as I saw a bridge coming up I climbed away to about 150 feet then, diving with my camera gun aimed at the bridge, I would sideslip heavily across to the other side of the railway, where I would straighten out at 50 feet until I saw the next bridge. Then I repeated the process back to the other side again, and so on. There must have been fifteen or sixteen bridges. After a while I started to notice tiny mushroom balls along the upper surface of the wings. There was an awful lot of dust on the plains of Burma, but I wondered how it could accumulate like that on the wings. At about the last bridge before Mandalay, out of the corner of my eye I saw five or six more of these little mushrooms spring up one after another in a straight line and I realised that we were being fired at the whole time. In Europe I was used to seeing tracer bullets; nothing was ever fired without tracer. But the Japanese either did not have, or did not use tracer, so one could not see where the firing came from. I flew back to Khumbigram and as I taxied in to my dispersal I heard the Australian ground crew sergeant's voice coming through my open cockpit window. 'What the bloody hell have you been doing? This is my plane and there must be four hundred holes in it for us to repair before tomorrow.'

Back in the Interrogation Room I thought I would mention it to the flight leader. 'Oh,' he replied, 'I'd have thought it was quite obvious to anybody that those bridges would be well defended. They always are you know. Glad they didn't get you.'

My next operation, to destroy a railway bridge but leave the road bridge next to it intact at a place called Thawatti, called for a technique I had not seen before: skip bombing. This involved dropping the bombs very low so that they hit the ground horizontally and then bounced in the air for about 100 yards until they came down and blew up. There were three of us. The first two did a magnificent job, rather like a 100 yard approach to the pin at golf. They made a bad mess of the railway bridge. I was next. As in golf, it is not as easy as it looks, and I blew the road bridge to bits.

On another occasion we had finished our bombing job and were on our way home when the flight leader decided that we should strafe a village pagoda with our cannon. Whilst I thought it sacrilegious, to pump a whole lot of shells into a pagoda, that is what we did. Back at base, one of the Australian pilots came across to me, furiously waving one of the camera gun photographs. 'What the hell do you think you were doing?' he asked, flourishing the photograph in my face. I looked at it, and was rather pleased to see that my aim appeared to have been pretty good. 'What do you think that is, bozo?' he said pointing to an aircraft a half mile in front in the upper part of the picture. 'That's me and your ricochets could have hit me!'

One day, when we could not get back to base, we stopped off for the night at a landing strip in the plains called Thazi. There was a big sleeping tent but we had to put our bunk beds well away from the sides, as otherwise we would be silhouetted by the kerosene lamp hanging inside and the Japs had been known to creep up silently and put a knife in people's backs through the tent canvas whilst they slept. In the evening we ate at a long refectory table. Opposite me was an army major, eating raw carrots mostly. I noticed from his signet ring that his name was also Braithwaite, Duncan Braithwaite. He turned out to have been a forestry ranger before the war, and as far as I could gather, had been fighting his own sabotage war against the Japanese for ever.

One of our problems at Khumbigram – and over the whole of India – was the vast number of vultures that were constantly wheeling around. If an aeroplane hit them, it could cause serious damage, even bringing a plane down. One evening, the flight controller was standing at the top of the control tower, and in exasperation at the 'shite hawks' as they were called, pulled his 45 colt revolver out of its holster and emptied it at them. Then, more relaxed, he lowered it whilst he surveyed the scene in front of him. There were no dead birds but then, his forefinger gave the gun trigger another little pull for luck, and a bullet which was still in the magazine went off and passed straight through his penis. He was rushed to the station hospital, and we were all greatly concerned. Flight Lieutenant Bamford came into the mess and I asked him if the man would live. 'Live!' replied Bamford. 'Of course he will, but what is more, when he's recovered, he'll be the most popular man east of Suez – he'll have an enormous lump on each side of it!'

Leonard Slee arrived at the station. 'Nice to see you again, sir,' I said. 'But, I've come a long way from Texas and here I am, back on Mosquitoes, with a fairly unfriendly crowd, and I can't help noticing that I'm still a squadron leader, with another Squadron Leader, who was here before me, thinking he should be the commanding officer,'

'Yes, sorry about that, Denys,' he replied, 'but you see they moved me from the job in the Arakan and I couldn't help it. With your experience, they insisted on sending you here. Incidentally, your telegram to Wing Commander Hazleman in the Air Ministry has done the trick again. You have your new navigator on the way out now. He's a flight lieutenant with three DFMs. You asked for the best available and it sounds like you've got him. I'll see what can be done about your promotion, but in the meantime I understand 45 Squadron is very short of crews – six isn't it?'

'Yes, mostly from hitting trees when attacking stupid things like gharries.' Gharries were small horse-drawn vehicles that it was presumed were transporting Japanese.

'Well, get down to Calcutta and go to see Wing Commander Lohmeyer there. Then go on to Yelahanka in Mysore where our reserve Mosquito crews are arriving and chose six replacement crews.'

I was at that time rather unwell – in fact the only place I was comfortable was in my seat in the Mosquito. I could not even tie up my own shoelaces. I was due to go on an operation the next morning, so I arranged to do it in order to give the medicine Bamford had given me extra time to work before leaving for Calcutta.

It was a 7.00 take off, so we were out at dispersal with the sun still trying to get up over the mountains in the east. Whitcutt decided he needed to go to the latrine before getting into the plane. I watched him disappear into the trees. All of a sudden, there came the most unusual and rather funny sight: Whitcutt, with his Bermuda Shorts below his knees running back as though he was trying to break the world 100 yards record. Breathless, white and shaking, he described how he had just got comfortably settled down on the wooden lavatory seat when he chanced to look to his left to see at elbow height, a cobra with its hood up giving him close examination. He had not waited and I do not think he needed to go to the lavatory any more. I can't remember what we did on the flight.

I got down to Calcutta feeling very unwell and reported to Wing Commander Lohmeyer. He took me down Chowringee to the Bengal Club, and when we had a couple of John Collins' in hand, he started off. 'Right, first as of today you are commanding officer of the lead Squadron at Madras, and you can go and get your wing commander stripes after lunch – or you can take mine if you like, I have another pair at home.'

'Having given you that good news, I'll tell you what it's all about. Even before you left England, you were never going to join Leonard Slee in his fighter wing. You have been chosen to lead the 120 strong Mosquito strike wing on Penang and then on to Singapore, and, even possibly, on to Tokyo after that. You have been up at Khumbigram to get a little experience that we could not have given you down here, as nobody here is operating on ground strike now. There'll be about six squadrons, of which 45 Squadron will be one, and another will be the lead squadron. It's all part of H Force and we could not tell you before as it was – and still is – completely secret. Incidentally, your group captain in charge of all air operations will be Leonard Slee and his Senior Officer is Air Vice-Marshal Coryton who used to be his Air Officer Commanding 5 Group from where Slee came to take over 139 Squadron that you were in with him. How does all that sound to you?'

'Absolutely splendid, but I think I had better go to Yelahanka first and get the crews. Then I'll go back to Khumbigram to pick up my things, and I'll put up the stripes after that if it's all right with you. I'm a bit superstitious.'

I did not feel up to flying to Yelahanka and I thought it would be easier to go by train. At Madras I had to change, which I found a painful exercise. At Bangalore I had to take a taxi out to Yelehanka. When we got to the main gates the taxi refused to go any further, saying it was forbidden. I got out and started to walk, but when I reached a banyan tree after about a hundred yards I sat down in the shade, unable to walk further. Presently a car came along and a squadron leader asked me what I was doing. 'Right,' he said 'I happen to be a doctor and I'll give you a lift if you will come to the hospital and be examined before you do anything else. Otherwise, I'll just have to leave you where you are,' I accepted.

I was told I had a severe case of dysentery and they would fix me up in no time. Several days later, after many unpleasant and uncomfortable tests, half the hospital brass came in. 'Squadron Leader, we've come to congratulate you. You have sprue and are going home to England,' they announced with enthusiasm.

'Firstly,' I said, 'what the hell is sprue. Secondly, I don't want to go back to England; I am probably the only person in this whole station who does not want to go home.'

Sprue, it turned out, was a particularly virulent and long-lasting intestinal disease, so I did go home. I never got to command my new squadron, and I never got to be a wing commander. Hitler's war was over before I left hospital, Hirohito's ended whilst I was still an invalid. In retrospect I enjoyed every minute of my time in the RAF and I shall never have future memories as poignant again, either of the living or the dead and I thank them all in perpetuity.

APPENDIX ONE

AGAINST TWO F.W. 190'S.

Mosquito aircraft P/521 Squadron (Pilot: S/Ldr. Braithwaite ; Navigator: Sgt. Davis) on "PAMPA" patrol from BIRCHAM NEWTON to NORDHORN and HAMBURG, was airborne from BIRCHAM NEWTON at 1705 hrs. 4th. September, 1942, and crossed the Dutch coast about 10 miles N. of IJMUIDEN flying at 28,500 feet on a course 106°T.

Immediately after crossing Dutch coast pilot altered course to 060°T. for about 20 miles and then altered course again to 106°T., which would have brought him over IJSSELMEER coast at ENKHUIZEN.

The object of this manoeuvre was to avoid enemy interception (through R.D.F. plot).

When approaching area of ENKHUIZEN at 1740 hrs. on a course 106°T. at 28,500 feet climbing at 160 m.p.h. (i.a.s.) crew of P/521 sighted 2 aircraft (subsequently definitely identified as F.W. 190'S) at a distance of 2000 yards on dead reciprocal at same height. Pilot took no evasive action until enemy aircraft, which immediately climbed slightly and spread fanwise, were almost in position for simultaneous quarter attack. He then went into a vertical aileron turn diving under enemy aircraft on starboard side (220°T.). This split up enemy aircraft and left only the enemy aircraft which had been approaching on port side in position (to carry out an astern attack). This latter was now watched by observer and a steep turn to port at the right moment caused him to overshoot.

Observer of P/521 had immediately on sighting enemy pulled up armour plate, kneeling on his seat facing to rear of aircraft and holding on with both hands (under considerable strain during evasive action) to armour plate handles. He was able to keep watch through perspex, blisters and, on pilot's side of aircraft, through the same by putting his head behind W/T set. The keeping of a constant lookout by the observer in this manner enabled him to keep pilot informed of every manoeuvre by the enemy.

Pilot had opened up to full revs. and boost, but not emergency boost in order to avoid risk of engine failure due to maintained strain. (See also Note 'E' at end). Aircraft was brought down to rated altitude (22,000 feet).

Enemy aircraft attacked in turn after first attack, one diving to attack while other climbed for position. During these attacks, as in most subsequent

attacks, determined endeavours seem to have been made by enemy to approach
to attack P/521 on pilot's side. In one attack enemy aircraft fired
purposely on the outside of P/521's turn giving the impression that he was
hoping to catch P/521 on the reverse turn (which pilot of P/521 was careful
not to make).

Evasive tactics (after the first attack) consisted of slight banking
turns (to enable observer to cover whole field of flight of enemy aircraft
to the rear and to keep pilot informed), followed by vertical turns always
towards enemy, coming out at somewhere between 180° and 270° around, and
alternately reversing these vertical turns, or steepening them, until high-
speed stalls at 260 to 280 m.p.h. (i.a.s.) developed, causing aircraft to
whip over upside down with all controls " juddering" fiercely, followed by
momentary loss of control during which nose dropped slightly allowing speed
and control to be rapidly regained and aircraft to be thrown into vertical
turn either side (continued until aircraft was heading into sun and towards
own coast) and then to be straightened out. This high speed stall was in
the first instance made unintentionally, but proved so successful that it
was employed at least six times.   During steep turns observer was compelled
to fold up on the floor and was unable to move due to centrifugal force. On
aircraft straightening out, however, he was able to rise and resume watch for
next attack.

Observer took pains (necessitating keen judgment and greatest
restraint) to wait until enemy aircraft was "in range" and its sights dead
on P/521 and obviously about to fire before instructing pilot "turn your
side" or "turn my side" as case might be. "Port" and "Starboard" were not
used in this emergency in case of error in the excitement of the moment.
Crew considered this delay to the very last moment before giving instructions
to pilot to turn as being very effective tactics as enemy aircraft was unable
to follow in close turns made by P/521 especially the closer and faster he
approached.

When about 5 minutes had elapsed from the time of the first attack
one of the enemy aircraft which had been successfully out-turned in the course
of a manoeuvre was seen to dive vertically out of sight. It is thought that
the pilot may have blacked out and lost control in a high speed stall. This
took place approximately over ALCMAAR at 22,000 feet.

The remaining enemy aircraft continued the pursuit carrying out a dozen or so attacks during the next 25 minutes during which tactics as above were mostly used.

P/521, during a lull, then came down to 9,000 feet, employing gentle fish-tailing in a fairly steep dive westwards into sun. Level of 9,000 feet was chosen as it is generally considered that this is probably best height at which to out-manoeuvre F.W. 190 aircraft and, as the difference in performance of enemy aircraft and that of Mosquito at latter's rated altitude left much to be desired, no experiment was considered unworthy of trial.

At 9,000 feet however the attacks seemed to become more frequent and evasion less satisfactory; pilot of P/521 therefore descended to about 2,000 feet. At this point (about half way across North Sea) enemy aircraft was seen on reciprocal 1000 feet above apparently about to turn for another dive attack, but enemy maintained course and was not seen again, due perhaps to ammunition shortage or P.L.E.

P/521 landed BIRCHAM NEWTON 1845 hrs. Casualties to personnel - NIL except for cuts, bruises and strains. Damage to aircraft - 1 bullet hole in starboard tail plane (fired from pilot's side and from slightly above) and broken perspex on wing-tip due to air pressure.

NOTES

(a)   Whereas pilot of one enemy aircraft seemed to suffer black-out neither of crew of P/521 blacked-out, but observer suffered considerably from bruises, strains and vomiting.

(b)   At least 15 attacks were carried out altogether.

(c)   The i.a.s. of Mosquito was approximately 260 m.p.h. at 25,000 feet. F.W. was estimated to be considerably more at same height (they were possibly faster type than hitherto encountered). Maximum i.a.s. attained by Mosquito at rated altitude (22,000 feet) was 350 m.p.h. i.a.s. in gentle dive. (Note: approximately 15 m.p.h. gained by closing radiator shutters).

(d)   The accuracy of the interception (if it was such) may perhaps be accounted for by the fact that other aircraft (Bomber Command (Mosquitos) had been operating at 27,000 feet over RUHR area at about the same time as P/521 was approaching.

(c)   After first high speed stall port undercarriage
indicator read down.   Both pilot and observer mistook
"juddering" for bullet strikes.   Indicator reading was
therefore accepted and repeated attempts were made to
raise wheel.   This had the effect of making the pilot
consider that the enemy's apparent superiority of speed
was due to the above and was responsible for his not
attempting to run for it by using emergency boost.

G R Bellews

                                        F/Lt.,
      Station Intelligence Officer, Bircham Newton.

8th. September, 1942.

                    M O S T   S E C R E T

To :- S/Ldr. Braithwaite, No. 521 Squadron.
....

        With compliments of Station Intelligence Officer,
R.A.F. Station, Bircham Newton.

EVASIVE TACTICS EMPLOYED BY MOSQUITO AIRCRAFT

AGAINST TWO F.W. 190'S.

Mosquito aircraft P/521 Squadron (Pilot: S/Ldr. Braithwaite ;
Navigator: Sgt. Davis) on "TAMPA" patrol from BIRCHAM NEWTON to NORDHORN
and HAMBURG, was airborne from BIRCHAM NEWTON at 1705 hrs. 4th. September,
1942, and crossed the Dutch coast about 10 miles N. of IJMUIDEN flying at
28,500 feet on a course 106°T.

Immediately after crossing Dutch coast pilot altered course to
060°T. for about 20 miles and then altered course again to 106°T., which
would have brought him over IJSSELMEER coast at ENKHUIZEN.

The object of this manoeuvre was to avoid enemy interception
(through R.D.F. pilot).

When approaching area of ENKHUIZEN at 1740 hrs. on a course 106°T.
at 28,500 feet climbing at 160 m.p.h. (i.a.s.) crew of P/521 sighted 2
aircraft (subsequently definitely identified as F.W. 190'S) at a distance
of 2000 yards on dead reciprocal at same height. Pilot took no evasive
action until enemy aircraft, which immediately climbed slightly and turned

forwise, were almost in position for simultaneous quarter attack. He then went into a vertical aileron turn diving under enemy aircraft on starboard side (220°T.). This split up enemy aircraft and left only the enemy aircraft which had been approaching on port side in position (to carry out an astern attack). This latter was now watched by observer and a steep turn to port at the right moment caused him to overshoot.

Observer of P/521 had immediately on sighting enemy pulled up armour plate, kneeling on his seat facing to rear of aircraft and holding on with both hands (under considerable strain during evasive action) to armour plate handles. He was able to keep watch through perspex, blisters and, on pilot's side of aircraft, through the same by putting his head behind W/T set. The keeping of a constant lookout by the observer in this manner enabled him to keep pilot informed of every manoeuvre by the enemy.

Pilot had opened up to full revs. and boost, but not emergency boost in order to avoid risk of engine failure due to maintained strain. (See also Note 'E' at end).   Aircraft was brought down to rated altitude (22,000 feet).

Enemy aircraft attacked in turn after first attack, one diving to attack while other climbed for position. During these attacks, as in most subsequent

Appendix Two

Sir,

I have the honour to submit the following report concerning two incidents on an operation to Leverkusen on December I0th. I943.

I was flying on the Lattice Line, approx. 50 miles inside Holland, at 26,300 feet, indicated airspeed I85 Knots, ground speed I60 Knots, at 2675 revs. Visibility was excellent, the moon was full and well up on my port bow on my course of I07°M. I was leaving no contrails, but other Mosquitoes trails, though short, had been easy to pick up over the sea, at about 27,000 feet and above.

I was altering course slightly to starboard, at about II5°M when I saw a black shape come past on my port bow, opening away from me. I watched and it turned parallel at about 600 yards and 200 feet above me. I remained steady. Aircraft then turned across and passed about 400 yards in front of me, on about I50°M, crossing my path at about 30°. As it crossed, it appeared to turn even further to the South, giving the impression that it had lost me and was going South to search. However, it then steadied at approx. I00 yards, nearly parallel but opening away slightly. Not wanting to lose sight I altered course to I30°M and increased speed to I90 knots by losing 500 feet. He was leaving no trail; I therefore wasn't, being lower than he.

He continued to open from me to about 800 yards, very slightly ahead. When I had almost convinced myself that the vague spot of blackness I was trying to watch had vanished, it suddenly appeared again flying on approx. 095°M, or across me at about 35°, and showing considerably greater speed than me. I immediately turned on to I40°M, still at 26,000 feet. Aircraft closed rapidly and crossed directly over my cockpit about 200 feet above. He was still leaving no trails, and burning no lights, but was excellently illuminated in the glare of two very bright exhaust pipes under each engine; I think he was an ME 4I0. E/A carried on on same course whilst I turned further south, on to I50°, and dived to 24,500 ft. which height I stayed at. E/A exhausts were well visible for 250 - 300 yards, and he vanished altogether at 6-800 yards and was not seen again.

I believe E/A was getting good ground control, but was not equipped with AI. His tactic was to come up-moon to me, but with AI this should not have been necessary considering the range at which I could see him.

His original approach appears to have been put off by my alteration of course to the south, which suggests that he did not have AI, nor did he get a visual sighting and GC did not have time to inform him. On being told I was south of him he used his superior speed to pass over to the south side in front of me, possibly intending me to see him do it and myself turn north to get away and therefore give him a further chance to come in behind me, up-moon. Anyway, his second effort was again beaten in a way which suggests he was being controlled entirely from the ground.

After this, the twenty minutes left to the target were flown at 200 knots indicated, at 24/25,000 feet, and just before target a climb was commenced prior to starting the bombing run. My navigator had gone into the nose to sellect the bombs; no flak had been fired; A/c had reached 26,500 feet indicated (25,700 feet True). Suddenly, looking between the cockpit and engine nacelle downward, I saw a metal-like object disappear under the leading edge of the wing. Thinking it was another N/F, I shouted to the Navigator and turned hard to port, to see, clearly shining in the moon, three quite large balloons, not more than 200 feet beneath and packed too tight for an aircraft to have been able to pass between them. The Navigator got out of the nose only in time to see them very vaguely, and , worried lest there might be more about, I did not attempt to try to relocate them.

The run-in was then commenced at 27,500 feet, heavy flak was encountered for one minute before bombing and two minutes after, quite accurate. Other crews state that I was well on target when getting this flak. Assuming that correct, and remembering that there was an 80 knot gale from the East, it seems possible that these balloons were being flown from Leverkusen. From their proximity to each other it would appear that they might well have all been attached to the same cable.

The return was uneventful.

Note: as George Hodder was unable to confirm these balloons, and as there was an eighty knot wind blowing, this report was never confirmed till after the war was over, when it was learnt for the first time that the Germans had been flying high altitude cables with three balloons to hold them up; it is presumed that on this occasion the force of the wind had probably snapped the cable and what I nearly ran into was a set that had become unmoored and was drifting.

Index